Straight Down The Middle

Meditations
for
Golfers

Straight
Down
The
Middle

Meditations
for
Golfers

Jim Dyet

Circle Books

Winchester, UK
Washington, USA

First published by Circle Books, 2011
Circle Books is an imprint of John Hunt Publishing Ltd., Laurel House, Station Approach,
Alresford, Hants, SO24 9JH, UK
office1@o-books.net
www.o-books.com

For distributor details and how to order please visit the 'Ordering' section on our website.

Text copyright: Jim Dyet 2010

ISBN: 978 1 84694 709 4

A CIP catalogue record for this book is available from the British Library.

Design: Stuart Davies

Printed in the UK by CPI Antony Rowe
Printed in the USA by Offset Paperback Mfrs, Inc

We operate a distinctive and ethical publishing philosophy in all
areas of our business, from our global network of authors to
production and worldwide distribution.

CONTENTS

Desert Palms

The Front Nine . . .

1/ Golf's Great Outdoors

Whether digging divots or driving 300 yards, today's golfer will tell you a round of golf chases his cares away. And who can dispute the claim? Anyone who spends four or five hours on a golf course receives therapeutic healing there. Stress lifts off and flies far away, as if Tiger Woods had clobbered it with his incredible strength, flawless swing, and perfect timing. Even a bad day of golf beats a good day at the office. "It was fun," you'll hear departing golfers tell each other. "Let's do it again soon."

If you enjoy the great outdoors of green hills, tree-lined fairways, and idyllic ponds, you can identify with David, the shepherd boy who became Israel's king. Although he held a shepherd's staff rather than a golf club, he marveled at God's creation. "O LORD, our Lord, / how excellent is your name n all the earth," he mused (Psalm 8:9).

I have often fantasized about playing golf in my native Scotland. The history, hills, heather, and heath golf's birthplace would quicken my pulse and refresh my spirit. My fantasy may never materialize, but at least I can treasure my golf memories woven in North America. The courses on this side of the Atlantic may lack heather and heath, but they provide abundant scenic pleasures.

Golf course designers deserve credit for their uncanny ability to carve beautiful fairways and greens out of hills and valleys, but God deserves our utmost gratitude for having created those hills and valleys. His creative genius lies behind the breathtaking beauty of New England courses, blanketed by fall colors, Midwestern courses blessed with ponds and meadows, mountain states courses framed by towering snowcaps, and southwestern courses ringed by cacti and bathed in sunshine. No wonder stress lifts and thoughts of God's majesty settle into our souls when we play golf.

Let the scenic surroundings of a golf course transport your thoughts up and away from our frenzied world of economic instability, terrorism, crime, and catastrophes. Let them take you a way for a while from spreadsheets, sales quotas, product deadlines, and personnel problems. Echo David's song of praise: "O LORD, our Lord, / how excellent is your name in all the earth."

2/ Sunday Golf

The unthinkable happened in Scotland in 1592. A royal proclamation restricted golf to six days a week, making Sunday golf as nonexistent in Scotland as a wasted penny. Apparently the king wanted Scots and their pennies to attend church regularly.

Much to the relief of Scottish golfers, the ban was amended in 1618 to allow Sunday golf if players attended church first.

I doubt that a ban on Sunday golf today would increase church attendance. Despite Christian golfers love of fairways, greens, long drives, and short putts, we love God more than golf. Our commitment to our great God exceeds our commitment to the great old game of golf. Come Sunday, we'll be present for worship.

By attending church regularly, we honor God, encourage fellow Christians, maintain our credibility with our neighbors, and strengthen our relationship with God. Another plus for regular church attendance—no tee time is necessary!

3/ Bobby Jones and Calamity Jane

To own a replica of the Calamity Jane putter is to own a significant piece of American golf history.

Although the Calamity Jane putter had been on the market for a couple of decades, it did not become famous until Bobby Jones first used in 1920. Then, six years later, he replaced it with another putter, Calamity Jane II, which he used masterfully in ten major championships.

The U.S. Post Office set up a temporary postal station at the 1976 U.S. Open in Atlanta to pay tribute to Bobby Jones and his Calamity Jane putter. The station was named the Calamity Jane, Georgia Station.

Today, visitors to the USGA Museum may see Calamity Jane II, donated by Bobby Jones. Calamity Jane I has its home at Augusta National Golf Club.

There is nothing fancy about Calamity Jane. Probably this simple blade putter would never have achieved fame except for one thing: Bobby Jones held it in his hands, applied his putting genius, and used it to win championships.

God doesn't need multitalented, highly educated, wealthy, and stunningly beautiful people to serve His purposes. Anyone with a humble heart and love for Him will do just fine. Remember, He used a scrubby desert bush to display His glory to Moses (Exodus 3:1-6). He used one stone and a shepherd boy's slingshot to drop the defiant giant Goliath facedown onto the ground (1 Samuel 17:45-50). He used a widow's nearly empty pantry to sustain Elijah (1 Kings 17:10-16). He stretched a young boy's small lunch far enough to feed at least 5,000 hungry people so well that the disciples were able to gather twelve baskets of leftovers (John 6:1-13).

Any believer, who offers himself to God as an empty vessel, receives God's power and is able to serve His purposes. God delights to respond to our availability with His infinite ability.

4/ Joe Louis and I

A photo in my office shows Joe Louis, a sports commentator, and me. Joe and the sports commentator were playing golf. I was caddying for Joe. At the time, I was 14, and Joe Louis, the former Heavyweight Boxing Champion of the World, was everybody's hero. I considered it a privilege to be his caddy, and to this day I treasure his autograph and the photo.

Joe was good golfer. He hit long, low, straight drives, but had a tendency to "punch" the ball. He was also a gentleman.

Struggles face the Christian who endeavors to live according to the Bible. Trials and temptations might knock us down for the 10 count if it were not for the Lord's sustaining grace and our resolve to "fight the good fight of faith "(1 Timothy 6:12). I can assure you the "fight" doesn't slacken as we grow older, but neither does the Lord's promise to take care of us. He said, "My grace is sufficient for you, for My strength is made perfect in weakness" (2 Corinthians 12:9).

5/ Nancy Lopez: Role Model

If you called Nancy Lopez a role model, who would disagree? She is highly regarded by her peers, fans, golfers, and youngsters for her professional achievements, generosity, and kindness.

Nancy, born January 6, in Torrance, California, took up golf at the age of eight under the watchful eye and guiding hand of her father Domingo. She won her first tournament at age 12 and continued to win tournaments throughout her career. In 1987, she was not only the first Latino woman inducted into the PGA World Golf Hall of Fame but also the youngest woman to be inducted into it. She entered with 35 tour victories to her credit. Golf Magazine named her Golfer of the Decade for the years 1977-1987. At the age of 40, Nancy won her last tournament. It was the same tournament in which she posted the best score ever for a female golfer.

Young athletes are often disappointed by their heroes, some of whom say flat out they don't want to be role models, but young athletes who look up to Nancy Lopez as a role model have made the right choice.

Known for her humility, Nancy would surely admit she is not the perfect role model. We might search the world over for the perfect role model, but we would not find a worthy candidate. Jesus is the only one who lived a perfect life. He never entertained a sinful thought or committed a sinful deed. Even Pilate, who turned Him over to an angry mob for crucifixion, confessed he found no fault in Him (Luke 23:22). Hebrews 4:15 says He was tempted in every way, just as we are, yet He was without sin. The apostle Peter spent more than three years following Jesus in Judea and Galilee. He observed His deeds and heard His words. Recalling Jesus' earthly life and ministry, Peter wrote: "He committed no sin, and no deceit was found in his mouth" (1 Peter 2:22). The apostle Paul referred to Jesus as having no sin (2 Corinthians 5:21).

We cannot go wrong by trusting in Jesus as our Savior and choosing Him as our role model. Obviously, we cannot lead a sinless life, as He did, but we can become like Him in character and conduct.

Read Philippians 2:1-13 and Hebrews12:1-3 today.

6/ Golf at Fort Carson Army Post

When asked where I play golf in Colorado Springs, I respond, "Cheyenne Shadows." Actually, I play wherever I am invited to play, but Cheyenne Shadows seems to top the invitation list.

Located on the Fort Carson Army Post, near the base of Cheyenne Mountain, Cheyenne Shadows Golf Course is accessible only to those who pass through security at Gate 5. Presenting my driver's license, registration, and proof of insurance is a required procedure, as is the ritual of popping the hood of my car, opening the doors, and lifting trunk lid.

After clearing security, I pay a modest green fee at the clubhouse, meet my buddy, and together we load our clubs onto a golf cart and fall into a line at the first tee, where we are often paired with young soldiers. Before long, we tee off, and the adventure begins.

Although Cheyenne Shadows is a military course, we don't hit our golf balls left, right, left, right, left, right—at least we try not to.

One day, two young soldiers—one from Pennsylvania and the other from West Virginia—joined my buddy and me. They had recently returned from a tour of duty in Iraq and will return to Iraq in six months. Neither soldier complained about having to serve in Iraq, and neither soldier said he wished for an easier life.

Just a gentle reminder—Christians are soldiers—soldiers of the cross—yet many of us want to serve God only as advisers. A far-too-prevalent attitude seems to be, "I'm not available for any ministry that involves personal hardship or takes too much of my time or runs the risk of being unappreciated and unrewarded." Such soldiers are what C. T. Studd called, "chocolate soldiers." They melt when the heat rises.

One soldier's golf game fell apart at the fifth hole, and he became so frustrated and discouraged he retreated to his golf cart and pouted. Only the tactful encouragement of his soldier buddy persuaded him to resume play at the eighth hole. I'm happy to report the despondent soldier played well once again.

Another gentle reminder—soldiers of the cross can become frustrated and discouraged. Some may become so discouraged they drop out of Christian service. However, we can encourage them to "get back into the game." A pat on the back works far better than a callous rebuke.

"Let us encourage one another," Hebrews 10:25 admonishes. Let's spread encouragement around wherever we Christians interact with one another. As soldiers of the cross, we need to buddy up in our constant conflict with evil.

7/ Par-don My English

Sometimes the English language doesn't make sense. The words, good and hot, may have nothing to do with temperature. Far out may have nothing to do with distance. Space cadet may not identify a person studying to be an astronaut. A blast often refers to a good time, not an explosion. And grass may mean something entirely different from what we see on our lawns.

Often, the golf term par doesn't make sense when we apply it to non-golfing situations. A teacher may write on a report card: "Johnny's work has not been up to par recently." Taken at face value, this report would mean Johnny's work has been outstanding. After all if a golf score is not up to par, it is below par and, therefore, outstanding. A Father's Day card may read: "Dad, when it comes to fathers, you are far above par." Meant to flatter, the term far above par is hardly music to a golfer's ears. And who hasn't shrugged and sighed that a string of bad circumstances is par for the course. How can a string of bad circumstances be such a good thing as par for the course?

God's words, written in the Bible, are consistent with His character. He is truthful (Deuteronomy 32:4); His words are truthful. He is wise (Jude 25); His words impart wisdom (Psalm 119:98). He is faithful (Deuteronomy 7:9); His words are faithful (Psalm 119:86, 138; Titus 1:9). He is the author of peace (1 Corinthians 14:33); His Word is the agent of peace (Psalm 119:165). He is the Creator of life (Genesis 1:1); His Word generates spiritual life (1 Peter 1:22, 23). God says what He means and means what He says.

Read Psalm 119:97-104, and expect God's words to direct you in the right way. His words are par for the course any day and every day!

8/ Slow Golf

Likely, more Christian golfers have had their sanctification sorely tested by a slow foursome in front of them than by natural hazards—wide ponds, hidden creeks, and deep ravines. It just isn't spiritually invigorating to address a ball and at the same time see a couple of golfers emerge from a wooded area less than 200 yards ahead and then see two more pop up out of a bunker. That's enough grief to cause even a preacher to consider calling down fire from heaven on four heads.

And why do the slowest, worst golfers on the planet spend the longest time on each green? You've seen them. They line up a putt from all angles, and then stand motionless over a putt for what seems like eternity. Maybe they have watched too many golf tournaments on TV and think they have to devote more time than the pros to their putting. After all, they reason, you drive for show but putt for dough.

Here are some suggestions for coping with the slow-foursome syndrome:

- Lie down. And stretch out on the soft, green fairway grass. Breathe deeply. Gaze at God's magnificent, vast, blue sky. Marvel at His creative power.

- Practice your swing, aiming away from the foursome ahead. Now is a great time to develop a slower backswing.

- Determine not to rush your next shot.

- Compile a mental list of ten reasons to be thankful.

- Meditate on a familiar passage of Scripture.

- Pray for your pastor. At the moment, he may be facing a far more stressful situation than you are.

- Track your way through a log of memorized Scripture verses.

- Contemplate what matters most in life.

The Bible often tunes us in to what we might not want to hear but need to hear. Romans 5:3, for example, speaks clearly that tribulation develops patience. An illness, a job layoff, a leaky roof, or a scrunched car—or a slow foursome ahead— are just a few of the kinds of tribulations that build patience. However, God uses tribulation to slow us down and take time to communicate with Him.

9/ Victory Beyond the Bunker

Every golfer has been there: in a sand trap, behind a tree, in a gully, in a thick rough, in a bunker. At such times we can decide to sell our clubs, give them away, or relax, keep the head down, and play a recovery shot that our golf buddies will recall for a long time.

A plaque in a bunker in the rough, off the left side of the 17th fairway at Royal Lytham & St. Anne's in Blackpool, England, bears silent testimony to a historic and dramatic recovery shot. Playing in the 1926 Open Championship and tied with Al Watrous, Bobby Jones Jr. hit a 5 iron out of the bunker's sand. The ball sailed 170 yards over the rough and landed on the green, inside Watrous's second shot. Jones parred the hole. Apparently, Watrous was so unnerved by Jones's recovery shot that he three-putted and lost the championship and its $100,000 prize.

Sometimes in spite of our best efforts to follow the straight and narrow path God has marked out for us in His Word, we wander into a bunker, and feel like giving up. Fortunately, God grants recovery shots. Our greatest victory may lie just beyond the bunker.

Peter was determined to follow the Lord closely. Courageously, but self-confidently, he boasted he would never deny the Lord (Matthew 26:35). But later, when the Lord was arrested and subjected to an illegal trial, Peter denied three times that he was one of the Lord's followers. He failed to confess Christ even in the presence of a young servant girl (vv. 69-74). Peter had fallen into a bunker, and he might have stayed there a long time if our Lord wasn't such a master of recovery shots.

Following His resurrection, Jesus restored Peter to Himself and commissioned him to feed His sheep (John 21:15-17). Not long after this restoration, Peter preached to a massive crowd of Jews gathered in Jerusalem for the Feast of Pentecost. Three thousand in the audience responded by believing on Christ (Acts 2:14-41). Peter's greatest victory had occurred just beyond the bunker.

Hebrews 10:35 cheers us on to victory: "Do not cast away your confidence, which has great reward." No matter how impossible a challenge seems today, trust God to turn it into an opportunity to manifest His power. He can get you out of the bunker in fine shape.

The Back Nine . . .

10/ The 2008 U.S Senior Open

The 2008 U.S. Senior Open was played at the Broadmoor Golf & Country Club. It was a big deal! Although the tournament was scheduled for July 31—Aug. 3, tickets were scarce months in advance. The event poured millions of dollars into the local economy and showed off the scenic wonders of the Pike's Peak region to thousands of out-of-state visitors.

The Broadmoor course and the five-star-rated Broadmoor Hotel are as beautiful as they are famous. Presidents and entertainment celebrities have stayed at the hotel and played the course. Photos of them grace the walls leading to the hotel's restaurant area.

I stayed at the Broadmoor in 2007 while attending the Write for the Soul Conference. I served as a resource person for the many aspiring writers in attendance. However, I have never played the Broadmoor course. Perhaps I will be able to play it someday. Hope springs eternal in a golfer's heart.

A few years ago, I thought I would tee it up at the Broadmoor. After I had served Highway Baptist Church in Falcon, Colorado, as an interim pastor, the congregation gave me a generous cash gift and a gift certificate for golf at the Broadmoor. However, when I presented the certificate at the pro shop, I was told the certificate was good for merchandise but not golf. Broadmoor golf, I learned, is restricted to members, members' guests, and hotel guests.

So why didn't I play golf when I stayed at the Broadmoor during the Write for the Soul Conference? Two reasons: snow and cold. The conference was held in winter and even if the weather had been warm, the conference left no time for anything but meetings and appointments.

Before the Senior Open, things took a turn for the good, though. My golf buddy Mark called to say he had an extra ticket to the event. "Would you like to go?" he asked.

I like questions that don't require much thinking. "Of course, I would like to go."

I determined that the next time Mark and I played golf, I would buy him a brat and a Gatorade. I didn't have to wait long. After viewing the Open in the morning, we played at a nearby course.

Christian friendship is always a treasure (Philippians 1:3-5), but it's priceless on a golf course.

11/ Those Painful Penalties

In clubhouse conversation, someone invariable laments, "Penalties killed me today. If it hadn't been for the out-of-bounds penalty on the 8th, the lost-ball penalty of the 12th, and the penalty for moving my ball out of a bush on the 17th, I would have had a good score." Well, in spite of our lamentations, penalties have been in place a long time and will be in place as long as golf exists.

Our golfing forefathers must have believed that attaching penalties to our sport would challenge us to hone our skills. I suppose they had good intentions, but ouch, penalties hurt.

The game of life has penalties too. If we break God's moral laws, we not only offend Him but also hurt ourselves. His saving grace cancels the eternal penalty our offenses deserve, but the natural consequences of our violations can steal our joy, haunt our conscience, and keep us from receiving an eternal crown (1 Corinthians 9:27).

Israel's King David violated God's moral law by having an affair with Bathsheba and then arranging her husband's murder. Those sins brought imposing penalties. Guilt robbed him of sleep. He felt unclean. He lost the joy of salvation. He ached all over. His wrongdoing weighed on his soul like a ton of dirt. Finally, instead of trying to cover his wrongdoing, he confessed it contritely and sincerely, and God forgave him. But David's sins had set in motion a series of events that would trouble his family and his nation for years to come.

According to Proverbs 8, "wisdom" instructs us to make right choices, Verses 32 to 35 indicate we embrace blessing, life, and divine favor by choosing to live wisely. Verse 36 warns we wrong our own soul if we reject wisdom. The personal and family tragedies that followed David's transgressions would stamp "Case Proven" over Proverbs 8:36.

Penalties are real and painful. Trust God to help you play the game of life by His rules.

12/ Up in the Air about Devious Thoughts

A Christian couple in Colorado Springs operates Colorado Vertical Adventures, a business that books helicopter flights over tourist locations and also for special events. The company also offers one-hour prayer flights over the city free to pastors.

As pastors zoom over the city and their respective churches, they pray for both.

When I learned about the opportunity to pray from a helicopter, my devious humor took flight, and now I am up in the air over it. I should not have entertained any of the selfish thoughts that flew into my mind. I thought I could have the pilot fly over the golf courses I play most often. Above Cheyenne Shadows Golf Club, I would ask the Lord to remove the wide pond from the par 5 eleventh hole. It seems I always have to hit my second shot over it, but seldom succeed. Over Cherokee Ridge Golf Course, I would ask Him to move the Par 4 tee boxes about 30 yards closer to the greens. Those holes are far too long for a golfer my age. Cruising over Springs Ranch Golf Course, I would pray for the sand trap at the front left of the second hole to become a grassy area and for the wide ravine on the third hole to close and become part of the fairway. High above Pine Creek Golf Course, I would pray for the rugged ravine on the first hole to disappear. Also, I would pray that the trees guarding the approach to the green shrink into low-lying shrubs.

Again, I confess such thinking was devious, totally selfish, and theologically askew. Besides, Billy Graham may have been right to say a golf course the only place God doesn't answer prayer.

It's easy, isn't it, to pray with selfish motives? A person may want to win the lottery, become cancer free, gain a big promotion, strike it rich on a TV game show, or own a multi-million-dollar home. However, we should never ask the Lord for anything if our motive is selfish. Jesus taught us by precept and example to pray for God's will to be done.

Read Matthew 6:9-15 and 26:36-42.

13/ Cellophane Wrappers

As a teen working in a golf course's pro shop, I was impressed with the colorful appearance of the golf balls in our glass showcase. Penfolds, Titleists, Spaldings, U.S. Royals, and Dunlops came colorfully wrapped in cellophane, and each one sold for less than a dollar. Today, the price might be $25, $30, or more. Even an empty box that once held a dozen cellophane-wrapped golf balls may fetch nearly $100 today.

The bright wrapping certainly enhanced a golf ball's appearance, but it added nothing to its performance. Each ball's true value was determined by what it was after the wrapping came off.

God's Word instructs us not to judge a person's worth by outward appearance. When Israel demanded her first king, the people selected Saul strictly on the basis of his good looks. He was tall and handsome. If they had selected their first king on the basis of how he looked to God, they would have selected David, a man after God's own heart (1 Samuel 8:19-20; 13:13-14; 16:6-13).

James 2:1-5 rebukes those who judge others by their outward appearance, and insists God places the highest value on faith and faithfulness—spiritual qualities.

If people could gain God's approval by outward appearance, the Pharisees would have earned a triple-A rating in His sight. But God's gaze penetrated the Pharisees' robes and phylacteries and revealed their corrupt hearts. He accepted only those who believed on His Son—even beggars in tattered garments and lepers with ugly sores.

When God measures a person's worth, He puts His

measuring tape around the heart and not around a designer dress or tailored suit.

Read 1 Samuel 16:1-13.

14/ Golf at Kissing Camels

I played golf at Kissing Camels, one of Colorado's premier courses. A golf buddy had bid on golf for four at an auction, and won. He graciously included me in the foursome.

Kissing Camels sits on a mesa directly across from Garden of the Gods, a popular tourist attraction. A massive rock formation in Garden of the Gods resembles two camels kissing. Nearly every fairway offers a clear view of Garden of the Gods, Pike's Peak, and Cheyenne Mountain. But, as we played, we were also treated to a close-up look at deer herds and a coyote. A regal buck stared menacingly at us when we looked for an errant golf ball (not mine) in a stand of ponderosa pine.

Viewing the spectacular scenery and wildlife yesterday reinforced my conviction that the Creator is all wise, all powerful, and benevolent. What a wonderful environment He provided for us! But nature rests under a curse (Genesis 3:17, 18; Romans 8:22), and therefore doesn't rival the beauty and majesty of the original creation. However, when Jesus returns to Earth, He will restore the planet to Edenlike conditions (Isaiah 11:1–9; 35:1, 2). I can hardly wait to play a premier golf course then.

15/ Is It the Clubs or Something Else?

What a wide choice of clubs we face! If we had money to burn, we could buy every new, improved driver that comes along. The ads for new clubs draw us like ants to a picnic and almost yank money, checks, and credit cards out of our grasp. We fantasize about super long drives, straight iron shots, and one-putt greens. High-tech clubs can make our dreams come true. Or can they?

The truth is—and we all know it—even the best-manufac-tured clubs cannot play a good game of golf all by themselves. They may help us play better, but they cannot substitute for talent. And talent is due partly to natural athletic ability and mainly to practice, practice, and more practice.

Have you taken a good look at the state-of-the-art helps for Christian living that fill the shelves of Christian book stores? Attractively designed books, CDs, and videos promise to improve everything from finances to marriage, but as helpful as they are, they are no substitute for the power of the Holy Spirit. As we apply biblical principles to our walk with God and depend upon the Spirit for the wisdom and strength to handle daily challenges successfully, we develop skills for living.

Before becoming Israel's king, David showed that depen-dence upon God is basic to success. His father had dispatched him to carry food to his three oldest brothers army brothers. When he arrived at the front line of Israel's army, he saw the enemy, the Philistines, entrenched behind their champion warrior, the giant Goliath. A hulking nine-foot-tall trash talker, Goliath made the Israelites feel like pygmies. When he challenged the army of Israel to send a soldier to fight him, not one "pygmy" stepped forward.

But then, the young shepherd boy David arrived. Believing God would enable him to defeat Goliath, David volunteered to confront Goliath. Reluctantly King Saul accepted David's offer, and placed his own royal armor on him. However, David explained he had not had sufficient time to test the armor. So he took off the armor, and chose to confront Goliath with his shepherd's staff, a slingshot, and five smooth stones. The result? A carefully aimed stone and reliance on God took down the mighty giant and saved the day.

Zechariah 4:6 announces, '"Not by might nor by power, but by My Spirit,' says the LORD of hosts." The Lord's ability more than compensates for our lack of ability.

16/ If the Hat Fits . . .

My son and my older daughter bought me a really nice watch for Christmas several years ago. I especially liked it because it was a golf watch. Limited edition. Brown leather wristband. Recessed etching on the face—of a golfer, caddy, green, and flag—in gold. Elegant black lettering around the design boasts "FOSSIL AUTHENTIC." As the grandkids say, "It's cool!"

I wear that watch proudly on and off the golf course.

But a not-so-cool hat came with the watch. It's a green baseball-style cap, and it's hanging on a hook in the garage. I put it there when I carried the torn Christmas gift wrap to the trashcan, and it has been hanging there ever since. I just haven't had the heart to toss it out. After all, it was a gift from my son and daughter. What kind of dad would junk a gift from his kids?

So here's the problem. The hat, like the watch, says FOSSIL. Fossil watches are popular, but who wants to wear a hat that says FOSSIL? Can you imagine the stares and not-so-funny comments I'd get if I wore it? "Look at that fossil." "Did you see that fossil with the FOSSIL hat?" "Now there's a guy who likes to advertise his age!" No thanks; I can get along nicely without that kind of attention.

So the FOSSIL hat will stay right where it is in the garage.

Now, this Christmas, if my kids give me a golf hat that says "PAR MAN," I'll even wear it to bed!

Strange, isn't it, how we accept some gifts enthusiastically but considerate others inappropriate, even unwelcome? I guess that explains why gift exchange lines are so long the day after Christmas. Yet, God's gifts are always appropriate and welcome. You see, He knows exactly what we need, what suits us best, and what we can use. The apostle James wrote: "Every good and perfect gift is from above, coming down from the Father the heavenly lights, who does not change like shifting shadows" (James 1:17). The apostle Paul commented about the variety of spiritual gifts God gives to believers. He said, "We have different gifts, according to the grace given us" (Romans 12:6). Then he counseled us to use our specific gift faithfully.

Let's not hang our spiritual gifts on a hook somewhere!

17/ Swedish Smorgasbord of Accomplishments

At 5′6″ Annika Sorenstam isn't the tallest woman golfer in the world, but before retiring at the end of 2008 she frequently stood head and shoulders above her competitors.

Born October 9 1970 in Stockholm, Sweden, Annika attended the University of Arizona. In 1992, she was the World Amateur champion, runner-up at the U.S. Women's Amateur Championship, and the second-lowest amateur at the U.S. Women's Open. Two years later she was named LPGA Rookie of the Year. She went on to win 72 LPGA championships and capture winnings that approached $23 million.

Here are some impressive facts about Annika's sterling career:

- captured the Solheim Cup eight times from 1994 to 2007;
- scored the LPGA's all-time low round of 59 at the 2001 LPGA Standard Register Ping;
- earned the title, LPGA Tour Player of the Year, 1995, 1997, 1998, 2001, 2002, 2003, 2004, 2005;
- scored three LPGA career holes in one;
- was inducted into the Golf World Hall of Fame in 2003.

LPGA pros like Annika Sorenstam amaze fans and keep elevating golf to higher and higher levels of accomplishment. But righteous women in the Bible also amaze us. We applaud their faith and courage, and find some of them in the Bible's Hall of Faith, Hebrews 11. This roster includes Sarah, Moses' mother, Rahab, and "women [who] received their dead raised to life again."

Today, too, the remarkable faith of righteous women is apparent. We see it in our churches, home, workplaces, on mission fields, and wherever Christian women link faith, love, and kindness.

18/ Favorite Club

Almost any golfer has a favorite club, the one he feels most comfortable with. It may be his Super TNT driver or his loft wedge or his putter or his 5-wood. We all know a 1-iron is nobody's favorite. Cartoons sometimes feature a golfer sleeping in bed with his golf clubs beside him. I doubt that any golfer sleeps with his clubs, but he might not sleep well if he lost or broke his favorite club.

My favorite club is a 6-iron.   I was nine years old when I purchased my first club, a Robert T. Jones 6-iron. I paid $5 for it, roughly the amount of money I earned caddying for 7 rounds of golf. The 6-iron was a good buy, though.

While saving for a second club, I gave the 6-iron quite a workout. I closed the face and used a long grip for long shots, and opened the face and used a short grip and short swing for short shots.

In sand traps that guarded greens my 6-iron became a sand wedge. I laid the clubhead far back and used a flat swing to blast out.

To this day, my best chip shots have been 6-iron chips. Occasionally, one drops in and makes me profoundly pleased that I spent $5 wisely so many years ago.

Former evangelist Vance Havner used to tell his audiences, "God doesn't have favorites, but he does have intimates." He realized God shows no partiality (Acts 10:34), but He does maintain close friendships. He invites us to draw close to Him (James 4:8, and He encourages us to talk freely and openly with Him (Philippians 4:6; Hebrews 4:16). He wants us to know Him well (Colossians 1:10).

Abraham was one of God's intimate friends (James 2:23). When God tested Abraham's love, Abraham proved his love for God exceeded his love for his beloved son Isaac (Genesis 22:1-19).

Moses was another one of God's intimate friends. He and God had private conversations in Midian (Exodus 3—4), on Mount Sinai (chapters 19 and 40), and on Mount Nebo (Deuteronomy 34:1-6).

David, too, enjoyed an intimate friendship with God, and God called him "a man after My own heart" (Acts13:22).

A list of God's intimates would surely include Peter, James, and John, the inner circle of Jesus' disciples. The apostle Paul's name would be on the list too. Early in his new life as a believer, Paul spent more than three years getting to know God well in Arabia (Galatians 1:15-24).

Our work for God is important, but our walk with Him is more important. Time spent in fellowship with God is far more valuable than time spent any other way—even time spent on a golf course with your favorite club.

Read Micah 6:8 and Philippians 3:8-10 today.

Ocean Shores

The Front Nine . . .

1/ The Stops of a Good Golfer

Backspin is a beautiful sight. What can match the beauty of a well-hit ball biting into a green just beyond the flag and then skipping back and rolling toward it? Backspin is more than beautiful, though; it is a great stroke saver. Thanks to backspin, a golfer can loft his ball over a close-in bunker, land it on the green, and keep it there. Without backspin, many a shot has cleared a bunker, only to bounce, hop, and roll off the far side of the green and into a sand trap or down a hill.

Backspin results from hitting down on the ball before taking a divot. Having been struck that way, the ball spins counter-clockwise through the air. When it lands, the counterclockwise spin causes it to slam on the brakes and bounce backwards and come to an impressive stop.

When adversity strikes us—usually low and from behind—God often uses this to apply the brakes to our lives. Without those sudden stops, we might scoot past the place He wants us to be and then find ourselves in a mess. If God had not applied backspin to Jonah's life, Jonah would have found himself in much more trouble than he met inside the whale. God appointed the whale to save Jonah from drowning and to give him time to rethink and renew his relationship with God. Once Jonah had learned that it is always best to obey God rather than run from Him, the whale delivered a better and wiser Jonah onto dry land (Jonah 1:1—3:3).

The apostle Paul, too, experienced a beneficial stop in his life. When he tried to push eastward into Asia, God applied the brakes to his life, and then steered him in the opposite direction. As a result of God's backspin in Paul's life, Europe received the gospel (Acts 16:1-10).

The Lord directs the stops as well as the steps of a good person.

2/ Golf, Poor Kids' Style

Where I grew up, a golf course and country club divided two neighborhoods. My friends and I lived in what we considered the poor neighborhood. We identified the other neighborhood as the rich kids' neighborhood. The poor kids caddied for 70 cents. On a really good day we could caddy for 36 holes or carry two bags for 18 and earn $1.40. That was back in the 1940s. The kids who lived in the rich neighborhood didn't caddy. They didn't have to.

But caddying offered a unique opportunity to learn how to play golf. It also gave us caddies something to look forward to every Monday of the summer. Most of us were preteens or young teens who caddied to help the family income. So we couldn't afford to buy our own golf clubs. Instead, we asked the golfers we caddied for if we could borrow theirs. We promised to take good care of the clubs, clean them after playing, and return them to our respective lender's rack in the bag room. We would supply our own golf balls.

Our designated Monday tee times started at the first glimmer of daylight. Usually, a heavy mist blanketed the golf course, and the greens were so wet that our putts left trails from contact to cup. But we were on the course and having fun.

I often think about the trust and generosity golfers extended to young caddies every Monday. They settled for a simple thank you, but they deserved a lifetime of gratitude for helping a bunch of kids experience the thrill of driving straight down the middle and making some good putts. The memory of any bad shots taken between tee box and cup seems to have vanished as quickly as the early Monday morning mist under a summer sunrise.

Generosity and kindness are earmarks of an exemplary Christian life. Knowing that God showers the riches of His grace upon us should motivate us to give liberally to His work and to those who need a helping hand. Read 2 Corinthians 9:6-15.

3/ Golf and Relativism

How long would you put up with a golf partner who adhered to relativism and carried that philosophy onto the golf course? Probably not long. A relativist insists there are no moral absolutes. He believes each person is free to decide for himself what truth is.

So think about it. Golf is a game of absolutes. Its rules define what is right and what is wrong. Golfers are not free to decide such matters for themselves. Those who play golf by the rules submit to a higher authority than themselves. As much as they might wish no penalty were attached to a ball struck out of bounds, they take a penalty. When they lose a ball, they abide by The Rules of Golf and take a penalty. They do the right thing, as defined by The Rules of Golf.

If a relativist determined how he would play golf by applying relativism, his out of bounds shots or lost balls would be subject to his own standards of right and wrong. After hitting the ball out of bounds, he might say, "Who says I have to take a penalty? I will decide what is right for me. As far as I'm concerned, I can hit as many times as it takes to find the fairway, and count the final shot as one. And who says I have to take a penalty for a lost ball? I can drop another ball without incurring a penalty. No one has the right to dictate right and wrong to me."

Wouldn't it be fun to play with such a person? Of course not! Golf would lose its significance if players disrespected its rules. And life loses its significance when the culture rejects the Bible as the infallible standard of right and wrong.

In one of Jesus' prayers, He referred to the Bible as "truth." He didn't say it contained truth; He said it is truth (John 17:17).

We may not always appreciate the Bible's objective truth, but we will face bitter consequences if we replace it with our own subjective thinking. Proverbs 3:7 instructs, "Do not be wise in your own eyes. Fear the LORD and depart from evil." The same book of the Bible warns, "There is a way that seems right to a man, but its end is the way of death" (14:12).

4/ Thirty Thousand Golf Balls Can Be wrong

If your travels take you even close to Coeur d'Alene, Idaho, you must tote your clubs to the Coeur d'Alene Golf & Spa Resort. The course is both beautiful and challenging. Several holes play alongside the 26-mile wide Coeur d'Alene Lake, but the 14th plays into the lake. From tee box to the 15,000 square-foot floating green it's a 175-yard Par-3 you will never forget. Nothing but clear, blue water separates you from the green, and if you land on the green, you will receive a certificate— something you might just want to frame. Most golfers plunk two balls in the water before dropping one on the green to play four. So receiving a certificate really is quite an honor.

You won't see a "Cart Path Only" sign at the 14th. The only way to the green is by water taxi under the command of a Coast Guard-certified captain. He docks the boat at the green, and then players disembark to putt.

How many errant shots fall short of the green or land over it or plunk down to the left or right? Each year, about 30,000 balls are recovered from the lake. The number represents a whole lot of golfers who missed the target and incurred the penalties.

We all have goals we want to reach, but some of them may seem as unattainable as landing on the floating 14th green at the Coeur d'Alene Golf & Spa Resort. January 1, for example, we may set a goal of losing 10, 20 pounds or more by December 31, but by the end of February, we are ready to abandon all hope of reaching the goal. We blame our failure on the coworker who loads the break room table with donuts, or we blame it on too much out of town travel. After all, a few sweet snacks between high-carb meals helps to while away lonely hours. Perhaps we set a lofty financial goal for retirement, but as the years click by we get no closer to the goal. Inflation, few pay raises, medical bills, and numerous other factors make the financial goal as hard to hit as a floating green.

But one goal stands alone in ultimate importance, and we dare not miss it. It's the goal of leading a life that pleases God. Such a life demands personal faith in the Savior, and the discipline to say focussed on what God wants us to be and do. The apostle Paul compared his commitment to that goal to that of a marathon runner who stretches every muscle to cross the finish line. He wrote: "I press on toward the goal to win the prize for which God has called me heavenward in Christ Jesus" (Philippians 3:14).

The joy of receiving a certificate for landing your first shot on the 14th hole's floating green is awesome, but it falls far short of the joy of receiving God's approval for attaining the goal of a life that pleases Him.

5/ The Dreaded Inconsistency Syndrome

Like most occasional golfers, I lack consistency. I may birdie a hole but build a snowman on the next. Almost 60 years ago, when I was a teenager and played almost daily in the good 'ol summertime, I scored consistently in the high 70s. Yes, I used to be consistent, but as my wife would say, "Old man Usedto is dead and gone." Now that my age is somewhere in the 70s, my repertoire of excuses for high scores is running in the 70s too.

I won't share every excuse with you, but here are a few: Haven't played much lately. Bad back. Bad weather. A too-early-in-the-morning tee time. Bad toenail. Bad bounces. Bad eyesight. Slow traffic getting to the course. Slow foursome ahead. Slow greens. Slow digestion. Borrowed clubs. New driver. Too many pothole bunkers. Too many blind holes. Too many responsibilities. Lost my touch. Lost my rhythm. Lost my concentration. Lost my 6-iron.

Once, when playing nine holes with my son-in-law Brad, I was even par at the end of seven. Then the dreaded inconsistency syndrome set in. I triple bogeyed the 8th hole and quintuple bogeyed the ninth. Even my repertoire of excuses could not explain that disaster.

Inconsistency can wreck Christian living too. About the time we assume we have almost mastered the art of walking with God, we blow it. And we can't blame anyone but ourselves. Fortunately, forgiveness and help are available (1 John 1:9; 2 Corinthians 3:5).

Just as scoring well in golf depends on our playing well consistently—one good shot at a time—so scoring well in the Christian life depends on walking consistently with God, one good step at a time.

6/ I'd Rather Be Golfing

There you were, on your way to work, when a bumper sticker caught your eye. Its message, "I'd Rather Be Golfing," resonated with you, and you thought, "Amen." What golfer wouldn't rather be golfing than going to work? But a job, not golf, pays the bills, feeds the family, clothes and educates the kids, keeps the house in good repair, the spouse happy, and makes it possible to buy golf balls and pay green fees. If a person became so addicted to golf that he quit working, his finances would suffer, and so would his family.

In Scotland, around A.D. 1430,"golfe" or "the gouf" had become so popular that King James II of Scotland feared the pastime placed the country at risk in its ongoing war with England. He reasoned that his men were spending too much time chasing the "golfe" ball and too little time practicing archery. Poorly aimed arrows would pose little threat to Scotland's English foes. So the king persuaded the parliament to pass an act banning "golfe."

As Christians, our interests must be subservient to our divine Ruler. We must identify anything that jeopardizes our effectiveness in His service and place it lower on our list of priorities. Jesus challenged, "No one, having put his hand to the plow, and looking back, is fit for the kingdom of God (Luke 9:62). Colossians 3:1-4 nudges us gently but firmly to keep spiritual desires paramount in our lives.

As strange as it may seem, some things are actually more important than golf.

7/ Grounding a Club in a Sand Trap

If blasting out of a sand trap is not golf's most difficult shot, it surely ranks a close second. Many a shot has gone awry when launched from "the beach." It has been known to resemble either a drive or a dive. If a player strikes his ball cleanly and hard, it may take off like a rocket. If he digs too deeply, he may find that after the sandstorm settles, his ball will be resting close by, perhaps in the same spot but deeper.

A golfer who is new to the game my not know it is against the rules of golf to ground his club in the sand. Seasoned golfers may violate the rule out of fear, thinking the ball will misbehave if he doesn't ground his club. Neither ignorance nor fear will persuade golf's rules committee to amend Rule 13.4c of The Rules of Golf. The Medes and Persians didn't write the rule, but it is as unchanging as any law they did write. We need to get used to it.

In his letter to the Romans, the apostle Paul pronounced the whole human race guilty of breaking God's rules (Romans 3:9-23). The heathen had failed to live up to the light they had received through God's creation. Civilized pagans had failed to recognize their so-called moral standards fell far short of God's standards. The Jews, who possessed God's written law (including the Ten Commandments), had failed to keep it. All three groups, therefore, stood like convicted criminals in the court of divine justice and God wasn't going to change His rules to accommodate the guilty. The ugly truth is we are all sinners (3:23).

But there is good news. God forgives those who trust in His Son as Savior (Romans 6:23). In doing so, He cancels the penalty of our infractions (Romans 8:1). Nevertheless, we are not free to ignore or violate His rules, but we are free to obey God willingly and gladly. Read Romans 6 today. Think about God's grace for righteous living next time you feel like grounding a club in a sand trap.

8/ The Club Maker's Mark

I started collecting antique golf clubs in 1991. They are hand forged, wood shafted, and they predate 1935, the year I was born. When I started playing golf as a young caddy, I often used wood-shafted clubs that I borrowed from members of our country club. So I feel somewhat sentimental about my hobby. Finding an antique club at a flea market or antique store brings back a flood of memories.

Before 1890 blacksmiths made club heads by heating iron bars in gorges and then pounding them into shape by hand. By the turn of the twentieth century steam-powered hammers lightened the work, but the manufacturing process still required patience and skill. The British iron makers from the 1880s to the 1920s became known as cleek makers, and stamped their identifying mark called a "cleek mark" on their club heads.

I don't think a club manufacturer today would even attempt to earn a living by making clubs the old-fashioned way. He would go broke faster than a high-priced golf ball goes out of bounds. But the old-time club makers managed to put bread on the table and take pride in their work. Their cleek marks represent their good name.

Many collectors try to find a variety of cleek-mark clubs, and the fun of doing so is almost endless. A shepherd's crook marked on a club identifies its maker as Alex Shepherd who [plied his trade around 1915. Alex Patrick put a spur mark on his clubs between 1905 and 1915. Andrew Herd Scott, clubmaker for England's George V, used a crown and lion from 1911 to 1925. St. Andrew Golf Company used a stag mark from 1910 until 1925, when it introduced a sun mark. Gene Sarazen used St. Andrew clubs in the 1930s.

The list of cleeks could continue, but I will mention only a few more: a pipe, a hammer, a serpent, a flag, an anchor, a bear, a thistle, and a Scottish bluebell.

Ephesians 2:10 identifies every Christian as a product of God's workmanship. We were like scraps of iron before He salvaged us, put His hands on us, purged us of our sin, and began to forge and polish us into the image of His Son Someday, His forging and polishing will be complete, and we will fully resemble Jesus Christ (Romans 8:29; 1 John 3:2). Right now, we bear our heavenly Father's cleek mark; He stamped the Holy Spirit into our lives (Ephesians 1:13).

How apparent is it to those who know us best that the Holy Spirit lives in us?

9/ Selecting the Right Club

Only a novice would use a three wood to reach a green fifty yards away, but even an experienced golfer doesn't always select the right club. You may have heard a golf buddy lament, "I should have used a 6-iron. The wind in my face knocked down my 7-iron twenty yards short of the green. Or, "I overshot the green by thirty yards. Next time I'll use a 5-iron instead of a 3."

No doubt about it, a player can lower his score significantly by using the right club at the right time, and Christians can turn in better scores in Christian living when we use the right Scripture in a given situation.

"Take the sword of the Spirit, which is the word of God, Paul wrote in Ephesians 6:17. Do we know the Bible well enough to be able to draw upon a specific truth for a specific temptation, trial, or decision? Jesus did.

When the devil tempted Jesus in a variety of situations, Jesus countered each temptation by quoting a relevant verse of Scripture. Read Matthew 4:1-11 to see what the temptations were, and then read Deuteronomy 8:13, 6:16, and 6:13 to see what Jesus quoted in response to the temptations. A Christian who knows the Bible well can follow the example Jesus set and, by doing so, deflect temptation.

Read Psalm 119 carefully and prayerfully, and make a mental note of all the benefits that accrue to the believer who meditates on God's Word and obeys it.

The Back Nine . . .

10/ The Olde Stymie

Golf Magazine's Encyclopedia of Golf gives an interesting perspective on the contribution of the Dutch to golf's development. It describes the Dutch people's style of play and certain words they attached to their game. It seems the Dutch were playing golf as early as the thirteenth century. Although they played on ice initially, hitting a ball at a post, they eventually introduced holes as targets. Their word put, meaning hole, may have given birth to our English word "putt." Also, a Dutch player would cry stuit mij when an object stood in the way of his reaching a hole. Our word "stymie" may have originated from stuit mij.

Various kinds of stymies may confront a golfer. Trees, of course, are the most common stymies. Having to hit from behind a tree has raised many a score and temper. Of course, stymies may confront us on greens too. Soft spike marks and scuffmarks are considered stymies if they lie in the line of play. A player may eliminate such stymies by repairing them, but he may repair old hole plugs and ball marks.

Stymies confront us in our walk with God. They are obstacles that lie between His goals for us and us. A desire to be rich by any means may be a stymie. A harmful relationship may block our way to a spiritual goal. And what about a desire to be "top dog" in our field of employment? According to golf's rules, a player cannot remove a stymie—like cutting down a tree—but a Christian can remove stymies by exercising faith and maintaining proper priorities. Moses pushed stymies aside in his pursuit of God's goals for his life, didn't he? Hebrews 11:24-29 credits him with pushing aside worldly prestige, sinful pleasures, vast wealth, Pharaoh's wrath, and the Red Sea in His pursuit of the mission God had placed before Him.

What stymies will we remove by faith today?

11/ What a Revolting Development!

William Bendix, who played Chester A. Reily on "The Life of Reily," a popular radio show in the 1940s and TV show in the 1950s, often found himself in a troublesome situation. That's when he would exclaim, "What a revolting development!" If Bendix were alive today and looked at a once scenic golf course southeast of Colorado Springs, he would most likely shake his head an say again, "What a revolting development!"

Before the course closed in 2009, it attracted avid golfers daily. The green fees were reasonable, and the course was modestly challenging because a creek ran across many of the fairways and ponds were abundant and crystal blue. The developer who purchased the course had planned to upgrade the course and clubhouse and add 260 home sites nearby. But his plan went awry, and the property is in foreclosure.

Those who bought homes adjacent to the course expected property values to increase and their golf course views to stay pleasant. After all, the Front Range of the Rockies lies just to the west. The Rockies haven't lost their grandeur since the foreclosure, but the course has been overrun with weeds, and the ponds have dried up. It is indeed a revolting development. One can only hope the property comes out of foreclosure and receives the tender loving care that can restore it to its former condition.

The human condition enjoyed better days, when Adam and Eve shared pristine nature in the Garden of Eden. Their surroundings were beautiful and peaceful. Best of all, they experienced God's presence and recognized His voice. But one day they disobeyed a simple command God had given them, and what a revolting development ensued. They lost their innocence, fellowship with God, immortality, peaceful surrounding, and marital bliss. Just as the course in foreclosure needs to be restored, so all the descendents of Adam and Eve need to be restored spiritually. Fortunately, Jesus accepted the assignment to restore us. He beautifies the life of everyone who trusts in Him, and He brings new life, peace, and fellowship with God.

Read Ephesians 2:1-10 today.

12/ Putting Tips from the Master

The autumn 1933 issue of Esquire included a number of putting tips given by the old master of putting, Bobby Jones.

- A light grip, with the grasp concentrated in the three smaller fingers of the left hand. The right hand controls touch and speed, but only the first joint of the right hand touches the club.

- A comfortable stance. Jones stood with his knees slightly bent. He insisted each player must find the stance that is most comfortable to him or her and not insist on reproducing another's stance.

- Rhythm and smoothness. The motion of the swing must create a feeling of ease and comfort.

- Arms resting close to the body. Jones stood with his feet close together and his arms close to his body. His right forearm lightly touched his pants, but his left arm was free to keep the putt on line.

- A long, sweeping stroke. Jones started the putter back close to the ground, along an imaginary line drawn through the ball to the hole. He used the left hand for direction and the right hand for touch and speed.

Bobby Jones was truly a master of the greens, and his putting tips are as valuable today as they were in 1933.

Like good putting, becoming a more effective Christian

demands spiritual skills and constant practice. We learn those skills from Jesus, the master of life, by reading the Gospels. Matthew, Mark, Luke, and John show us how Jesus prayed, did the Father's will, taught, responded to His critics, and changed many lives. Thanks to the Gospels, we can sit at the Master's feet and learn from Him.

13/ Allowing for the Wind

Windy conditions challenge golfers. Hitting into a strong headwind toward a green that lies just beyond a big pond, players who use less club than they need will likely make a big splash on that hole. Players approaching a green with the wind at their backs will most likely play their next shot to the green from the opposite direction. Hooks, draws, slices, and fades are subject to the will of the wind unless players know how to allow for it.

Selecting the right club is crucial to playing well in windy conditions. You may need to add one club for every 10 mph headwind. You may need to hit a low shot into a brisk headwind. Tee your ball slightly lower than usual, play it back in your stance, and don't try to kill the ball. To take advantage of a tailwind, tee your ball a little higher than usual, play it slightly ahead of your left heel, and swing normally. When facing a left-to-right crosswind, a draw shot is probably your best strategy. Using a light grip farther down the club than usual, direct your swing inside the target line and keep it fairly flat. To compensate for a right-to-left crosswind, use a fade shot. Take an open stance wind, swing back outside the target line, and cut across the ball.

The book of Acts reports that the Church was born in windy conditions. As the believers prayed together in an upper room, the sound of a rushing wind filled the room. The Holy Spirit filled the believers, enabling them to speak in foreign languages they had not learned. Soon, thousands of Jews who had traveled to Jerusalem from many Mediterranean countries to observe religious holidays were hearing about God's wonderful works in their native languages. Three thousand listeners believed on Christ in one day.

The Hebrew word for Spirit, rauch, means wind or breath. The Greek word for Spirit, pneuma, also means wind or breath. Just as the Holy Spirit used the first-century believers at Pentecost to persuade many to believe on Christ, so today He uses believers to persuade men, women, young people, and children to believe in Christ. But the individual believer must obey the command to be filled [controlled] with the Spirit (Ephesians 5:18). Those who resist His control miss the productivity, joy, and peace that result from the Spirit's power. A life lived under the Spirit's control exhibits the Christlike qualities listed in Galatians 5:22 and 23. Meditate on these verses today, and allow for the Wind.

14/ A Courageous Golfer

Heather Farr, a native of Phoenix, Arizona, was tough emotionally and mentally, a strong competitor, and a true champion. Twice, she was all-American golfer at Arizona State. At twenty, in 1986, she became the youngest player ever to qualify for the LPGA Tour. LPGA player Mary Bryan commented that when Heather first joined the tour "nobody worked harder. Heather was determined to do well. She was a very feisty young lady."

And Heather did well—very well. In three and a half years she won more than $170,00 and her future looked as bright as the Arizona sun. But then tragedy struck, and Heather faced a challenge much tougher than the LPGA Tour. She learned July 3, 1989, she had breast cancer. Later that year she reflected: "You go through life, especially as an athlete, thinking you're doing all the right things with your body. You never expect this to happen". (The Chicago Tribune, 20 November 1993).

In 1992 Heather remarked regarding cancer, "You play through it, that's what you do."

Regrettably, Heather died November 20, 1993, but until her death she maintained a will-not-concede attitude in spite of 15 operations, including a radical mastectomy, a bone marrow transplant, and spinal surgery. She was 28 when she died.

The Chicago Tribune reported that more than 20 golf pros demonstrated their love and respect for Heather by being present at Scottsdale Memorial Hospital-North when she passed away.

According to the Bible, life is fragile and uncertain. No one can predict what will happen tomorrow—or even ten minutes from now. Whether sunshine or rain enters our lives, we need courage and faith to play the course God has designed for us.

15/ North America's Oldest Golf Course

North America's oldest golf course sits on the shore of Lake Ontario and welcomes golfers as it has since 1875. Niagara-on-the-Lake Golf Course hosted the first ever international tournament September 5-7, 1895. The event included a longest drive championship in which golfers teed it up on the first hole and gave it their all. Charles B. Macdonald of the Chicago Golf Club won both the tournament and the longest drive. His drive traveled 179 yards, one foot and 6 inches. Likely no one referred to Macdonald as "Big Mac," but it would have been a fitting nickname.

I grew up in the Niagara region and enjoyed playing Niagara-on-the-Lake when I was a young teen. You can imagine my delight in returning to the course a few years ago after an absence of almost 60 years. The trees and fairways were still lush and the scent of the Lake Ontario was still invigorating. Fort Mississauga, a prominent course landmark was still standing, a bit more weather-beaten but just as impressive as ever. Constructed during the War of 1812, the all-brick fort replaced nearby Fort George and helped in the defense of Upper Canada.

My return to Niagara-on-the-Lake brought back not only many memories but special joy as well. My son-in-law Brad, who accompanied me from Denver, Colorado, and my brother Bruce of St. Catharines, Ontario, played the course with me. As I recall, it was a fairly even match, although a couple of times I felt like hiding in the fort.

In recent years I have played North America's highest course, Mt. Massive in Leadville, Colorado, and North America's oldest course, Niagara-on-the-Lake. Before I die, I would like to play North America's easiest course.

Keeping memories alive of pleasant experiences, like playing Niagara-on-the- Lake when I was a kid, is therapeutic. If we store enough good memories in our mind, there will not be much, if any, room left for negative memories. The psalmist encouraged us to remember the Lord all the good things He has done for us. He wrote in Psalm 103:2: "Praise the LORD, O my soul, and forget not all his benefits." And he gave us a good reason to do so now. He said, As for man, his days are like grass, he flourishes like a flower of the field; the wind blows over it and it is gone . . ." (verses 15, 16).

16/ Loco for Logos

Anyone who sees racks of logo golf balls on my office walls might think I was loco—crazy. I'm not. I simply enjoy collecting golf balls with distinctive logos. My collection has a sports teams section: San Francisco Giants, Green Bay Packers, Chicago Cubs, Buffalo Bills, Chicago White ox, Chicago Bulls, Chicago Bears, Colorado Rockies, Denver Nuggets, Seattle Supersonics, and several more. I also collect golf balls with business and golf course logos.

I added the Chicago Bulls logo ball to my collection when Michael Jordan led the Bulls to their third NBA Championship. I hung my hat in Chicago during the Michael Jordan era. I treasure my Cherry Hills logo ball. Cherry Hills, Denver, is where Arnold Palmer won the 1960 U.S. Open, snatching victory from the jaws of defeat. Denver was my home from 1971 to 1990.

I picked up a Gleneagles logo ball in Manchester, Vermont, when I was conducting a prophecy conference nearby. It features a bright green eagle. The fall foliage at the Gleneagles course was spectacular when I purchased the logo ball.

My Mickey Mouse logo ball silently challenges me to improve my game. Mickey Mouse golf belongs only in cartoons.

A majestic red rock jutting up into a deep blue sky adorns the Arrowhead Golf Course logo ball. If you visit Denver, bring your clubs and play Arrowhead for unforgettable experience. A downhill 179-yard par 3 carves a narrow canyon path to the green. Scrub oak and tangled bushes flank the path to the green, a sand trap lies in front of the green, and a pond lies behind the green to swallow balls that golfers hit too far.

As diverse and numerous as logo balls may be, their

diversity and number can't compare to the diversity and number of believers scattered around the world. Yet, for all our differences, each of us is distinct and cherished by our heavenly Father. He has collected us into His family. He knows us by name and thinks about us every moment of every day. Our logo may be Bill, Jim, Jesse, Jose, Tammy, Tom, Gene, Gordon, Mark, Mary, Hernando, Hans, Brenda, Bob, or some other name, but He calls each s His child.

God has stamped His logo on your life. Carry it humbly and display it clearly.

17/ Putt for Dough

"Drive for show. Putt for dough." It's an old adage, but it is still true. A 1995 news photo showed Jack Nicklaus smiling and giving the thumbs-up sign after sinking a birdie putt worth $50,000.

Most golfers can only guess how they would react to winning $50,000 for sinking a putt. If it happened to me, not only would my thumbs be up, my arms and feet would be up too. It might be quite a while before my feet touched ground again. Yes, winning $50,000 would give me quite a lift.

Many of life's greatest joys, though, aren't linked to money. Not even $50,000 can match their value. For example, what can equal a significant answer to prayer? How can parents measure the worth of seeing their children walk with God? Good health is a gift from God and is worth far more than $50,000. In the absence of good health, God's sustaining grace is priceless. And didn't Jesus teach that the total value of all the world's resources is less than the value of one soul? Also, nothing is more valuable than our Savior's daily fellowship. With deep emotion and understanding the Christian can sing:

I'd rather have Jesus than silver or gold,
I'd rather have Jesus than riches untold . . .
I'd rather have Jesus than anything
This world affords today.

No wonder the apostle Paul counseled the Philippian Christians to rejoice in the Lord (Philippians 4:4).

18/ Bogey Coyote

When two golf buddies and I walked off the 18th green of Springs Ranch Golf Course in Colorado Springs, we saw a fierce-looking coyote positioned between the cart path and a pond. I'll call him, Bogey Coyote. Crouched and facing the pond, Bogey appeared big and mean. However, after staring at him for a while from a safe distance, we noticed he wasn't moving. Surely he didn't die in that position, I thought.

One of my golf buddies threw an old golf ball at Bogey, but Bogey didn't move. We took a closer look, and discovered Bogie was a fake—a lifelike fake, but a fake nonetheless.

When we asked the pro shop attendant why Bogey was positioned beside the pond, he replied, "We put him there to scare away ducks and geese, and it has worked. You didn't see any ducks or geese at the pond, did you?

Ducks and geese may not be able to tell a real coyote from a fake—until a real one bites, but you and I should know the difference. However, how often do we fear something that cannot harm us? Our Bogey Coyote may be one of a host of what-ifs that may never become real. What if I get cancer? What if I lose my job? What if I get involved in a car wreck? What if . . .

Such fears may keep us from living confidently with reliance upon God and His promises. Philippians 4:8 commands, "Do not be anxious about anything, but in everything, by prayer and petition, with thanksgiving, present your requests to God." Verse 7 identifies the result of turning our anxieties over to God: "And the peace of God . . . will guard your hearts and your minds in Christ Jesus."

If you face your fears with faith, you will find they can't hurt you any more than Bogey Coyote can hurt geese and ducks. So don't be a silly goose!

Soaring Eagles

The Front Nine . . .

1/ Course Etiquette

Golf has been referred to as a gentleman's game, because etiquette is an essential part of the game—at least it ought to be. Almost as soon as a golfer learns the difference between a driver and a putter, he discovers the importance of course etiquette. Here are a few course etiquette rules:

- Don't cheat.
- Remain quiet and still when a player addresses his ball.
- Don't laugh or even grin when a player muffs a shot.
- Replace divots.
- Don't hit out of turn. The player who is farthest from the hole hits first.

The player with the lowest score on a hole hits first off the next tee box. (He has the honors.)

- Stand out of a player's line of vision when he hits.
- Don't step on the "line" between a player's ball on a green and the hole.
- If your ball lies in a player's line on a green, remove it and mark the spot where it lay.
- Allow a faster group to play through. When all members of your group have reached a par-3 green, stand behind the green and signal the next group to hit.
- Don't hold up play.
- Don't hit your ball until the group in front of you is well out of reach.

In life, as well as golf, Christians ought to practice etiquette. Jesus, our example, was kind and considerate, wasn't He? As His followers, we, too, should be kind and courteous. Philippians 2:4 exhorts us to put others' interests ahead of our own, and Jesus instructed us to do to others what we would want them to do to us (Matthew 7:12).

Galatians 5:22 and 23 list nine traits called "the fruit of the Spirit." At lest three of those traits relate to etiquette. They are love, kindness, and gentleness. We can deliver baskets of these fruits where they are often needed most—the golf course.

2/ The Mighty Mulligan

A mulligan is a bad tee shot that doesn't count, Without penalty, a player gets to hit a second tee shot and forget the first one happened. Although a mulligan isn't allowed under The Rules of Golf, among friends it is often in the unwritten sacred code of fellowship. Generally, friends agree to allow each player one mulligan per nine holes except on a par 3. A less generous agreement permits a mulligan only on the first tee.

I don't know where I would be without the mulligan. Okay, I confess—I do know. I would be 30 feet off the tee box or in deep rough or out of bounds or in a pond.

Please don't think I need a mulligan on every hole. I don't. But a mulligan sure comes in handy once or twice during every eighteen holes. One or two mulligans can drop some fat of an unsightly score.

No one can say with certainty how the mulligan originated. Some golf historians claim it began when someone showed kindness to an Irishman with a wild golf game. As a Scotsman, I am quite certain the mulligan did not originate in Scotland. The Scots are rather legalistic about golf. Besides, if it had origi-nated in Scotland, wouldn't we know it as the MacMulligan?

One thing is certain—the mulligan is a product of sheer, undeserved kindness. It can't be earned; it can only be received. It is golf's grace gift.

Christians know and appreciate grace. We are saved by God's grace, and His grace supplies all we need to lead a joyful and productive life. Under the "rules of law," none of us deserve salvation or divine care, but in love God extended grace to us and drew us into His forever family. Because Jesus died for our sins and rose from the grave, God has freely erased our sins and given us a fresh start.

Why not read today what Ephesians 2:1-10 says about God's amazing grace?

3/ Out of Bounds of the Law

My wife and I rode Amtrak from Chicago to Denver several Christmases in the early 90s. Christmas lights and decorations in Kewanee, Illinois, projected charm and good cheer. It seemed to be a typical, friendly Midwestern town. But one of Kewanee's citizens proved to be untrustworthy and criminal. While casting himself in the role of a friendly neighbor and squeaky-clean Sunday school attendee, he committed 85 burglaries.

"Mr. Friendly" even taught Sunday school, dropped in on neighbors for a howdy-do chat, invited folks to lunch, and struck up a golf-buddy relationship with a number of local golfers. However, his neighborliness was a sham, a smoke screen that gained ready access to Kewanee homes he eventually burglarized.

During each neighborly visit, the Sunday school teacher learned where the residents kept their valuables. At friendly lunches he would excuse himself, hurry to the home of the person he was having lunch with, burglarize it, and then rush back to finish lunch.

The Kewanee burglar's golf buddies fared no better than the other victims. "Mr. Friendly" would arrange a golf game but arrive late for the tee time. While a golf buddy waited for him, "Mr. Friendly" was rummaging through the unsuspecting victim's home and carting off his valuables.

A golfer who cheats on the course runs afoul of The Rules of Golf, but a golfer who burglarizes his buddy's home runs afoul of the rules of civility. He is out of bounds of the law.

Ultimately, "Mr. Friendly" got what he deserved. As he exited a house, police caught him red-handed holding a stash of valuable coins. Once the burglar was in custody, life in Kewanee returned to its normal neighborly ways, and golfers returned to punctual tee times.

Judas Iscariot, one of Jesus' disciples, pretended to be Jesus' friend. He traveled with Jesus, listened to His parables and sermons, and shared meals with Him. None of the other disciples suspected Judas's friendliness was a guise. They never guessed he would betray Jesus. But Judas did just that for the sum of 30 pieces of silver.

Unlike the Kewanee golfers who were deceived by their buddy's feigned friendship, Jesus knew what Judas was planning to do. "One of you shall betray me," He told His disciples at the Last Supper (John 13:21). Even when Judas kissed Jesus in the Garden of Gethsemane Jesus perceived the kiss to be a kiss of betrayal. He has always been able to distinguish His true friends from those who simply want to get something from Him.

Friendship is a sacred trust. Real friends help one another, support one another, and pray for another. True friends are always welcome in Kewanee—and everywhere else.

4/ Golf Partners

Golf partners may not look like a matching set. They may not play like a matching set, but their fates and fortunes are inextricably bound together for four or five hours. Together, in that brief segment of time, they try to outwit, outplay, and even psych out their opponents. If they win, they congratulate each other. If they lose, they console each other, and each claims sole responsibility for the loss.

Golf partners ride together or walk together, and as they do so, they strategize. They celebrate each other's fabulous shots and commiserate over the flubbed ones. When one has a bad hole, the other is likely to come through with flying colors to save the hole.

During the game partners blend their skills, battle the course, and bond their souls. When the final putt clinks in the hole and the scores are tallied, they recall the best shots and excuse the worst. Then, after a hot dog, they go their separate ways, and each is better prepared for the challenges he must face alone.

The Bible applauds partnerships: Moses and Aaron; David and Jonathan; Elijah and Elisha; Peter and John; Paul and Silas; Priscilla and Aquila. A good partnership of believers works wonders for both. As iron sharpens iron, so a friend sharpens his partner (Proverbs 27:17). As Solomon wisely observed, two are better than one, because if one fails, the other can help him get back on his feet (Ecclesiastes 4:10). Also, two can defend against a foe better than one (v. 12). These are a few good reasons to develop a strong partnership with a fellow Christian. If you already have such a partner, give thanks and do your part to help your partner succeed in the Christian life.

5/The Five-Minute Rule

I am Scottish born, but I would rather abandon a lost golf ball than hold up play. I know what it is like to play behind a foursome that searches for a lost ball as though it were worth a million dollars. If only every search party obeyed Rule 27 of The Rules of Golf! It declares a ball is "lost" five minutes after the player's side or his or their caddies have begun to search for it.

The human soul is infinitely more valuable than even the most expensive golf ball, and it lost condition is far more serious than that of a lost ball. Fortunately, God doesn't limit His search of a lost soul to five minutes. Sometimes, He searches throughout a lost soul's entire lifetime. As a matter of fact, God has been seeking lost souls since the first human beings sinned in the Garden of Eden. Genesis 3:9 reports that, after their tragic sinning, God called out to Adam, "Where are you?" Indeed, throughout history God has been searching for the lost and calling out to them. Revelation, the last book of the Bible, records God's relentless call to the lost to return to Him. "And the Spirit and the bride say, 'Come!' And let him who hears say, 'Come!' And let him who thirsts come. Whoever desires, let him take the water of life freely" (Revelation 22:17).

The Rules of Golf allows others to assist a player in searching for his lost ball, and God allows us to assist in the search for lost souls (2 Corinthians 4:3–6; 5:19, 20). Once a person is found, God restores him progressively to a perfect condition—to the flawless, unblemished, spotless image of His Son (Romans 8:29; 2 Corinthians 3:18).

6/ Home, Home on the Range

The pros spend a lot of time on the driving range, and the rest of us should too. But it is often one thing to know what we ought to do and another to actually do it. Televised coverage of golf tournaments often show the pros warming up on the driving range before their respective tee times. And where do they go after they play. Right—back to the driving range.

One of my friends hits a large bucket of balls from a driving range before every game. Another friend practices his putting on a practice green. I don't do either one, and my lack of practice shows on the first few holes. As a type A person, I like to cut to the chase, so to speak. I show up to play golf, not to practice golf.

But I have another excuse: a bad back. I have had two extensive lumbar surgeries that have limited my ability to swing a club repeatedly without developing leg cramps. So I save the swings for the game. And stooping over a ball for long on a practice green causes my sciatica to flare up.

Pretty good excuses for not practicing, don't you agree? If you disagree and can offer a better excuse, I would be happy to add it to my repertoire.

I am sure my game would improve if I took time to prepare properly, but golf is just a game. No eternal consequences stem from a couple of triple bogies per round. However, living is more than just a game. If we do not prepare properly for each day's challenges, we can't expect to build successful relationships, defeat temptation, and fulfill God's will.

How did Jesus prepare for the challenges He encountered? He arose long before daybreak, found a quiet place, and prayed there (Mark 1:35). Prayer prepared Him for the busy ministry of preaching and healing. His preparation also included the acquisition of thorough knowledge of Scripture. When the devil tempted Him severely in the desert, Jesus warded off each temptation by appealing to a Scriptural command (Matthew 4:4, 7, 10). Soundly defeated by Jesus' resolute commitment to God's will, the devil slunk away.

If we want to lower our golf score, we need to practice, practice, and practice some more. If we want to resist temptation and lead a successful daily life, we need to read the Bible and pray every day.

7/ Beautiful Courses

Artistically designed golf courses are a delight to behold and a privilege to play. If you flip through a golf course calendar or view a painting of Augusta's Amen Corner (12th hole), you will definitely want to play those courses.

Golf architects, such as Old Tom Morris, Willie Park, Jr., Alister Mackenzie, Donald J. Ross, Robert Trent Jones, Paul "Pete" Dye, and Jack Nicklaus have graced the golfing world with courses carved from their knowledge and skill.

Jesus, the master architect of all creation, is preparing the New Jerusalem for our eternal occupancy. Upon completion, its glory will far exceed the glory of the world's greatest courses. Its beauty will surpass by far the beauty of their fairways and greens. Best of all, Jesus will reveal Himself to us as "the King in His beauty" (Isaiah 33:17).

As you anticipate the splendor of your eternal home, offer praise to the One who is preparing it for you. Everything He does is perfect, and therefore He cannot build a less than perfect home for His followers. Our eternal home will never need repairs. It will never experience a power outage. It will never grow old, break up, or fall down. It will always be bright, comfortable, and environmentally sound. New Jerusalem's huge wall will rest on twelve jeweled foundations, and it will have twelve pearly gates. If you are like most Christian golfers, you must be hoping it also has eighteen emerald greens.

8/ Nice While It Lasted

In 1959 my wife gave birth by C-section to our first child. The pregnancy had been rough, and required more than usual number of doctor visits. My salary as a pastor was hardly enough to put food on the table and gas in the car for the frequent pastoral visits I made in rural Canada. But back then pastors were more highly respected as the Lord's servants than they are today. Besides, very few pastors commanded large salaries, lived in luxurious homes, and drove swanky cars. So doctors often gave pastors a sizable discount. Some refused to charge for their services. Neither the general practitioner, nor the anesthesiologist, nor the surgeon charged a single penny for the medical care they gave my wife and our first baby.

As years passed, pastors' salaries increased, and so clergy discounts started to fade into oblivion. As late as the early 1980s, though, I enjoyed a huge golf discount. The city and county of Denver, Colorado, issued certificates to resident pastors that allowed them to play any city-owned course for just $2. The certificate cost only $5 and was good for an entire year.

Frankly, I don't know of any clergy discount that exists today. Oh well, it was nice while it lasted. Playing a round of golf for just $2 was a little bit of money well spent!

Not much is free, is it? The business community often says, "There is no such thing as a free lunch." Somebody is always looking for a bigger favor than he invested in the lunch. But the greatest benefit of all is totally free—no strings attached. It is God's gift of salvation, purchased for us by His Son at the cross, and received by faith. Romans 6:23 tells us "the gift of God is eternal life in Christ Jesus our Lord."

9/ The Ten-Second Rule

Your putt is right on the money. It is glorious. You watch it roll right to the center of the hole. But it stops a hair width short. Maybe, if you stomp on the ground, the ball will drop. Or perhaps a breeze will emerge from nowhere and blow it into the hole. You wait, and you wait. Like a frightened first-time skydiver frozen in time at the plane's open door, the ball appears to be indecisive. Will it take the plunge or stay where it is?

According to The Rules of Golf, a player can wait ten seconds for the answer. If the ball drops into the cup within ten seconds of its coming to rest on the edge of the cup, it is determined that the player made the putt. If it drops into the cup after the ten seconds, the player must add another stroke to his score.

Ryder Cup player Sam Torrance was stung by the ten-second rule on the European Tour in 1990. He waited 27 seconds for his ball to drop from its precarious perch atop a hole. When it finally dropped, Torrance exulted, believing he had made a 3. Bad news soon reached him: he had waited too long. His score was 4.

God's patience is enormous, but it isn't limitless. He waited 120 years in the days of Noah for humans to repent. However, when the 120 years expired, He destroyed the unrepentant human race. He waited four hundred years before He sent the Israelites into Canaan with a mandate to utterly destroy the wicked Canaanites. He extends His patience today, but no one knows when He may withdraw it and judge nations that defy Him. Proverbs 27:1; 29:1; and 2 Corinthians 6:2 warn unbelievers about the risk of presuming on God's patience. Now is the right time to turn to God.

The Back Nine . . .

10/ "Get in the Water!"

Phil Mickelson led Nick Watney by one stroke going into the 18th hole of the WGC-CA Championship at Doral, Florida, March 15, 2009. Phil had never won a WGC championship, and doing so would not be easy. Watney proved to be a formidable opponent, to reach the narrow fairway a player must hit a long drive over water, and Phil was sick. He had been sick and dehydrated for three days. To add to his woes, just as his drive took flight, someone in the gallery shouted loudly, "Get in the water!" One of the announcers commented that a fan like that should be escorted abruptly off the course. However, Phil did not show any anger; he simply went about his game. He and Nick scored pars, and Phil had won his first WGA championship.

Courtesy and respect seem to have been slipping away from professional sports—at least on the spectator side of the action. Streakers have rushed onto football fields; drunken football fans have thrown snowballs and beer at opposing-team players; unruly hockey fans have littered the ice with debris when they disagreed with a penalty; and occasionally an out-of-control baseball fan has rushed an umpire. Soccer matches have erupted in mob violence. But golf has been spared such outlandish acts. Nevertheless, rude verbal outbursts may escalate into obnoxious overt behavior someday.

Christians should pursue a life of respect and kindness. The Bible admonishes us to "put on tender mercies, kindness, humility, meekness, longsuffering" (Colossians 3:12), and "above all these things put on love" (v. 14). We should conduct ourselves as Jesus' followers.

11/ The Little Cart That Couldn't

When I was an editor at Cook Communications Ministries, my boss and I occasionally took a day off for golf. One day we rented a golf cart that didn't run well. It sputtered and palpitated before it rolled along each cart path. Fortunately, the course was flat. This cart would definitely not carry two golfers from hole to hole on a mountain course.

Surprisingly, our golf cart chugged along for twelve holes, but when we were about 20 yards off the 13th tee box, it coughed its last breath. My boss suggested I steer while he pushed in a desperate effort to jumpstart the cart. But it resisted his valiant effort. To make a bad situation worse, it had given up the ghost at the farthest point from the clubhouse, and neither my boss nor I had a cell phone.

I scanned a row of houses along the north side of the fairway and found a teenaged boy sitting in his backyard. He kindly let me use a telephone to call the pro shop and report the demise of our cart. And then my boss and I removed our clubs from the back of the cart and did what every golfer used to do in the old days—we carried our clubs and walked. Two holes later, a pro shop attendant delivered a fresh cart to us.

Does it seem to you that trouble usually strikes at the worst possible time, perhaps when you feel your situation is hopeless? Moses and the Hebrews could have felt like that. Soon after fleeing Egypt, they came to the Red Sea. How to reach the other side and continue their journey to the Promised Land? They faced what appeared to be an unsolvable problem, but soon the problem intensified beyond imagination. Pharaoh's cavalry was hot on their heels. They could not go forward, nor could they retreat.

But God is bigger than the biggest problem. Neither Egypt's military power nor the Red Sea could thwart the plan He had drawn up for His people. God's servant Moses commanded the Hebrews to stand still and see how the Lord would deliver them (Exodus 14:13).

And now the rest of the story . . . God carved a path through the Red Sea. The Hebrews followed it to the opposite shore, but when the cavalry pursued, the waters returned, and the Egyptians drowned.

A dead golf cart did not ruin a day of golf, and apparent insurmountable problems will not ruin our lives if we turn them over to God.

12/ Bee-ware!

Next time you reach for the open can of pop you placed in the golf cart's cup holder, check it out before you chugalug its contents. A golfer in Schaumburg, Illinois, died suddenly after picking up and taking a big swallow of pop from an open can.

Here's what happened. While the golfer was putting, a bee was attracted to the sweet scent of pop and crawled into the can for a sip. When the golfer returned to the cart and swallowed some pop, he also swallowed the bee. It stung him in the throat. He experienced an allergic reaction. His throat swelled shut, and he died before help could arrive.

I think about that tragedy often when I drink a can of pop on the golf course. It is one thing to stay hydrated, but quite another to get stung. A bee is just a small creature, but it can end a life.

Have you noticed how abruptly a person may shrug off a sinful habit if he or she thinks it is just a little sin? The excuse usually goes like this: "What harm can an occasional binge cause?" "So I fly off the handle once in awhile. It's no big deal." "I admit it: I pad my expense account a little, but I don't rob banks or snatch purses from little old ladies. Nobody's perfect!"

But a little wrongdoing isn't harmless. Nor is it little in God eyes. He declares in Proverbs 8:36: "But he who sins against me wrongs his own soul." Even a little sin can block answers to prayer. The psalmist wrote, "If I regard iniquity in my heart, the Lord will not hear: (Psalm 66:18).

It pays to make sure a bee hasn't crawled into your pop can. It also pays to make sure a little sin hasn't crept into your heart.

13/ Rage Defused

There was not a chance of my second shot reaching the green. In my younger days I could have reached it, but like a home run ball, those days were long gone, and they weren't coming back. So the players on the green were safe; I could hit my 3-wood and hopefully come within 50 yards of the green and hope for a third shot that would give me a shot at a par.

My golf buddies assured me, "You're safe to hit, Jim."

I addressed the ball, took a slow backswing, connected, and watched in disbelief as my ball rolled onto the green. My feelings were a mixture of embarrassment and elation, but they soon turned to astonishment and anger. One of the players on the green picked up my ball, placed it beside the green, walked to his bag, picked out an iron, and hit my ball into a nearby creek. He had demonstrated not only poor sportsmanship but also rage.

He must have been surprised on the next hole to see me drive my cart alongside him at the spot of his tee shot. He might have expected me to confront him—to give him a piece of my mind for hitting my ball into the creek. But that is not why I caught up with him.

"Sorry I hit while you were still on the green," I said. "I'm a Christian, and I would never do something like that intentionally. I haven't hit a ball that far in years."

"And I'm sorry I hit your ball into the creek," he admitted. "I need to learn to control my temper."

We shook hands. He continued his game. I returned to the tee box, and determined to practice the art of patience.

"A soft answer turns away wrath, but a harsh word stirs up

anger," Proverbs 15:1 counsels. A humble apology can defuse rage both on and off a golf course.

14/ Neither Snow, Nor Rain, Nor Heat

We have all heard one version or another of the United States Postal Service's motto. Probably the most common version is: "Neither snow, nor rain, nor heat, nor gloom of night stays these courageous couriers from the swift completion of their appointed rounds." However, Herodotus, the Greek historian, first uttered these words about 2500 years ago, during the war between the Greeks and Persians. He was describing the Persian mounted postal couriers, whom he observed and held in high esteem.

Except for "the gloom of night" part, this ancient motto fits more than a few golfers. It certainly fits me and my golf buddies. We have played in all kinds of weather: extreme heat, cold, snow, hail, sleet, fog, and thunder and lightning.

Joe, a good friend who lives in Chicago, visits me occasionally in Colorado, and when he does, we play golf.

Summer days along Colorado's front range usually start with sunny, blue skies, but by mid afternoon, puffy white clouds begin to build over the mountains. By late afternoon they turn menacing black and spawn violent thunderstorms. Lightning streaks across the sky like angry bursts of long, jagged swords. Rain may follow briefly, but often the thunderstorms produce nothing but enormous booms and staggering lightning displays. One such afternoon, Joe and I were playing golf on a course just east of the Air Force Academy. When puffy white clouds grew big and inky above the Academy, we were playing the 17th hole. When we reached the 18th hole, the booms and pyrotechnics began. Flashes of lightning persuaded most golfers to seek cover.

Joe urged me to get into the cart and gun it for the clubhouse, but I was on my way to a good score. I know I put my life in peril, but I played on in the thunder and lighting. I wanted to complete the round and post a memorable score. I came close to posting a memorable scorch.

Let me say emphatically a golfer should seek shelter when lightning approaches, but some golfers play only when weather conditions are ideal. They are fair-weather golfers.

Fair-weather Christians exist too. They serve the Lord only when the conditions are comfortable. They refuse to take any personal risks. Yet, serving the Lord is not an option; it's a mandate. The apostle Paul instructed Timothy to proclaim God's Word "in season and out of season" (2 Timothy 4:2).

Can we be God's couriers even in snow, rain, heat, and gloom of night?

15/ It's All about the Short Game

How many times have you been only a few yards off the green on a par 4 in two shots but taken 6 for the hole? Too bad there isn't a rule that allows us to pick up the ball within fifteen yards of the green and add two more strokes for our score on that hole. It isn't going to happen! Even a 300-yard drive straight down the middle on a 365-yard hole may lead to a double bogey or worse if Mr. Smashem's short game is terrible.

Things can go terribly wrong after a long, straight drive. A topped ball. A shank. A sand trap burial. A ball can easily roll over the green, run down a steep slope, and come to rest in a clump of bushes. Three putts and even four putts can wreck a score.

In Christian living, too, it's important to have a good short game. A good start followed by a series of missteps can mar one's testimony. Little things such as controlling one's temper, speaking kind words, filing an honest tax return, giving an honest day's work, helping a neighbor in need, and treating others respectfully are essential elements in the short game.

Christian character isn't simply one booming accomplishment. It is made up of several qualities that show up in our closest relationships. Galatians 5:22 and 23 list them: love, joy, peace, longsuffering, kindness, goodness, faithfulness, gentleness, and self-control. These short-game qualities determine the effectiveness of our overall game of life.

16/ Massive Golf Fun

If you visit Colorado Springs in the summer and bring your clubs, you may want to invest a day in a unique golf experience. In less than three hours you can drive west to Leadville, an old mining town, and play Mt. Massive, a nine-hole course. But it isn't like any other nine-hole course; at 10,000 feet, it is North America's highest golf course, and it offers great views of several snow-capped mountains, including Mt. Massive. Colorado's second highest mountain, Mount Massive rises to a height of 14,421 feet.

My golf buddy Tom accompanied me to Leadville when I was scheduled to preach at a church there. After church, we played Mt. Massive Golf Course twice. The first nine served as a learning experience. We made smarter club selections during the second nine, and we had a better feel for the elevated greens. We discovered the thin air at 10,000 feet translated into greater flight distance than we were accustomed to at Colorado Springs' 6,200 feet elevation. We enjoyed longer drives than usual, and we often clubbed down two clubs. If you live at a low elevation, just think how much fun you will have playing golf at 10,000 feet— If you can breathe.

There is something invigorating about high-altitude golf. The ball travels farther, but the air is clean and fresh, and far from a noisy city, the high mountain environment is quiet. Elevating our thoughts and deepest desires to a high spiritual level is also invigorating. There is simply no substitute for withdrawing from the noise and stress of a busy life and drawing close to God through Bible meditation and prayer. The apostle Paul encouraged us in Colossians 3:1 and 2 to seek the things that are above and to set our minds on things above."

17/ Wounded Tiger?

A week after winning the U.S, Open in a 19-hole playoff in June 2008, Tiger Woods had surgery on his left knee. He missed golf eight months, but he roared back in March 2009 to win the Arnold Palmer Invitational at Bay Hill. He did so in dramatic fashion, coming from five shots back and sinking a 15-foot birdie putt on the 72nd hole to capture $1.08 million with a 5-under 275.

After winning in this stunning way, Woods' emotions took charge. He rushed into the arms of his caddie. The caddy showed similar high-intensity emotion by lifting Tiger off his feet.

What a comeback! What a celebration! Tiger's roar had been heard in the land again. But Tiger faced a far more serious challenge than knee surgery. He fell morally, and the fall cost him personal disgrace, his marriage, some endorsements, and the respect of many golf fans. Tiger apologized publicly and vowed to become a better person, but his game hasn't returned yet to its former level. It appears our Tiger is wounded.

The apostle Peter tumbled into disgrace. His fall didn't involve immorality, but it could have permanently destroyed his relationship with Christ. Peter had denied his Lord three times and then watched from a safe distance as He suffered an excruciating death on the cross at the hands of brutal soldiers. Where was the loyalty Peter had pledged so strongly to Jesus just days before he denied Him? He had fallen under the grip of cowardice. It looked like he would never recover. But he did recover and become a champion of the Good News.

Peter could not take credit for his recovery, though. He didn't spring into Christian leadership by self-will or self-effort. The risen Lord Jesus accomplished Peter's recovery. He met Peter beside the Sea of Galilee and commissioned him to feed and guard His sheep. Soon, the roar of this recovered apostle was heard in Jerusalem. Three thousand of those who heard Peter roar the Good News believed on Jesus.

It's good to know the Lord can recover fallen Christians.

18/ Barnstorming

Decisions on the Rules of Golf (© 1993, the United States Golf Association® and the Royal and Ancient Golf Club of St. Andrews, Scotland. Triumph Books, Chicago) offers everything a golfer would need to know about the game's rules. Perhaps, it gives far more than a golfer needs to know. For example it answers such questions as:

- What do you do if your ball lands near a rattlesnake or bees' nest? Are you required to play it, or can you consider it unplayable and take relief? (Answer: You may drop your ball without penalty in a safe spot but not nearer the hole.)

- What's the ruling if you have played your ball from off the green and a dog picks it up while it is rolling on the green and carries it away? (Answer: Place another ball without penalty as close as possible to the spot where the dog picked it up.)

- What do you do if your club breaks during your downswing, and you continue the downswing but miss the ball? (Answer: You must count it as a stroke.)

Here's my favorite. It will come in handy if I play a very rural course.

- Are you allowed to open barn doors to play a shot through the barn? (Yes. The barn is an immovable obstruction, but the doors are movable.)

What a complicated game!

In the first century, the Pharisees, a group of religious leaders, tried to impose hundreds of rules on the Jews, but they failed to keep them themselves. However, Jesus came to give life and liberty to all who would believe on Him. The Christian life is not a composite of complex rules; it is a life energized by the Spirit and guided by the principles of Scripture. "My yoke is easy, and My burden is light," Jesus said (Matthew 11:30).

Whispering Willows

The Front Nine . . .

1/ World Golf Hall of Fame Legend, Gene Sarazen

Gene Sarazen began caddying at the age of ten and died at the age of 97. He packed a lot of superb golf into his life and is remembered as one of golf's greatest golfers. At age 20 he won the 1922 U.S. Open and PGA Championship, and the following year he won the U.S. Open again. He won it again in 1933. He claimed the British Open in 1932 and the Masters in 1935.

With 39 PGA tournament wins to his credit, Gene was inducted into the World Golf Hall of Fame in 1974. He also played on six U.S. Ryder Cup teams, and received the PGA's Tour's first Lifetime Achievement Award in 1996. At 71, in 1973, he made a hole-in-one at the British Open Championship.

Perhaps Gene Sarazen is best known for two accomplishments. In the 1935 in the Masters Tournament, he hit "the shot heard 'round the world." It happened on the par-5 15th hole of the final round, when he was trailing the leader by three shots. His second shot, a 4 wood traveled 235 yards and found the hole. He went on to win the tournament in a playoff with Craig Wood.

Gene is also remembered well for inventing the sand wedge, which he called the sand iron and introduced in the 1932 British Open. Next time you pull out a sand wedge, think of Gene.

Living long, as Gene Sarazen did, does not guarantee lasting accomplishments, but it certainly provides numerous opportunities to do so. However, whether we live long or not, our lives should be dedicated to serving God. The apostle John lived well into his nineties and counseled, "he who does the will of God abides forever" (1 John 2:17). The apostle Paul did not live into the golden years, because an executioner's sword ended his earthly life. But Paul had committed his time on earth to his

Lord's service. Among his last words of Scripture were these: "I have fought the good fight, I have finished the race, I have kept the faith" (2 Timothy 4:7).

We may not be inducted into the World Golf Hall of Fame, but if we play the game of life well as believers, we can enter God's Hall of Faith.

2/ Battling the Wind

I have played golf in windy conditions—at clergy golf outings, for example (just kidding). At times, I thought a strong wind would topple my golf cart or blow me across the fairway when I tried to walk to my ball. However, in all my years of golf, I have never encountered winds like those that buffeted players in the 2009 Kraft Nabisco Championship in Rancho Mirage, California.

Defending champion Lorena Ochoa lost her balance in a gust of wind. Angela Stanford felt sharp pain rip through her ankle. But the wind caused even more damage to Ji Young Oh. Ji Young's ball was resting on the 18th green, when a wind gust blew it about 30 feet off the green and into a lake. Thanks to the wind, she incurred a one-stroke penalty. That's enough to blow a golfer's mind, isn't it?

Louise Friberg, Ji Young Oh's playing partner, also had a quarrel with the wind. One of her putts lipped out of the hole and rolled back 8 feet.

The Bible doesn't promise an unending succession of blue skies, sunshine, and calm conditions. Nor does it promise a gentle wind behind our backs. It promises some adversity and persecution will confront us as we try to walk by faith. In other words, gusty winds will threaten to push us off course. Jesus told His disciples, "In the world you will have tribulation" (John 16:33). The apostle Paul assured young Timothy, " . . . all who desire to live godly in Christ Jesus will suffer persecution" (2 Timothy 3:12). The apostle Peter wrote, ". . . when you do good and suffer, if you take it patiently, this is commendable before God. For to this you were called, because Christ also suffered for us" (1 Peter 2:20, 21).

In golf, the player who performs best in windy conditions captures first place and its accompanying prize. Similarly, the Lord will award a prize to all who faithfully overcome adversity (Revelation 2:10).

3/ Sing, Shake, and Splash

Brittany Lincicome won the 2009 Kraft Nabisco Championship, but she had to battle her nerves as well as her closest opponent, Kristy McPherson. As she forged forward, she and her caddie sang country songs to calm her nerves.

Going into the final hole, a 485-yard par-5, Brittany trailed Kristy by one stroke. She hit a 275-yard drive, and then selected a hybrid for her second shot. It sailed 210 yards before landing on the green just 4 feet above the hole. By her own admission, she said she was shaking to the point almost crying when she putted, but the putt dropped into the hole for an eagle and the championship.

Brittany was elated as she took the traditional victory plunge into the lake that surrounds the 18th green. She was the first American winner in the last six women's majors.

Singing is often an effective way to soothe the soul. Life brims with situations that threaten to unnerve even the staunchest believer. Rogue nations threaten our security. Crime runs amok. Jobs are tenuous. Inflation advances. Nuclear capability slips into the hands of nations bent on destroying us. And tomorrow is as unpredictable as a tornado's path. But singing can be thera-peutic.

Most of the psalms in the Bible were meant to be sung. King David wrote many psalms—songs— when his enemies hunted him relentlessly, hoping to kill him. He soothed his soul by singing when he was a fugitive from Saul. During that frightful period, David hid in caves and wandered in desolate, hot, dry, country.

Here are a couple of verses he must have sung to keep his

spirits high and his faith strong:

"Behold, God is my helper; The Lord is with those who uphold my life. He will repay my enemies for their evil. Cut them off in Your truth" (Psalm 54:4, 5).

"Cast your burden on the LORD, and He will sustain you; He will never permit the righteous to be moved. . . . I will trust in You" (Psalm 55:22, 23).

So, if you feel shaky in a tight situation, why not sing? A splash in a lake is optional.

4/ Hypocrisy on and off the Golf Course

My years of caddying taught me to count not only the strokes taken by the players I caddied for but to count the other players' strokes as well. Sometimes what I counted did not match what a player said was his score. My math was correct, but his ethics missed the mark. He was a cheater.

I'm sure we have all played golf with a cheater at one time or another. We know he had an 8, but he claimed a 6. We watched in amazement as he threw his ball out of the rough and onto the fairway without taking a penalty. His string of self-given mulligans on a hole made our eyes roll. He failed to take any penalties for lost balls or OB. We thought, If this guy ever gets a hole in one, he will write zero on the scorecard. At the end of the round, he congratulated himself on his low score. He was an expert in the fine art of hypocrisy.

The verb form of "hypocrisy" comes from the Greek word, hypocrinomai, meaning "to pretend or to make believe." In ancient Greek drama in the time of Plato, actors were called hypocrites, because they hid behind masks to play certain roles. So it isn't hard to see that cheating golfers are hypocrites—they pretend to be better golfers. They turn in make-believe scores.

Hypocrites carry their pretend game into many aspects of life. They pretend to give an honest day's work for an honest day's pay, when in fact they spend much of each day goofing off. They pretend to worship the Lord each Sunday by singing "praise songs" and dropping a donation in the offering plate, but they actually worship themselves or their possessions and give very little of both to the Lord. They mention God's name reverently at church but profane His name elsewhere.

We have all encountered hypocrites. Jesus knew we would, and compared them to "whitewashed tombs which appear beautiful outwardly, but inside are full of dead men's bones and all uncleanness" (Matthew 23:27).

Cheaters—hypocrites—need to recognize that God keeps accurate scorecards.

5/ Do Not Attempt This at Home!

Joe Kirkwood Sr. visited the course where I caddied as a boy. He was a golf trick shot artist who put on quite a show. I watched him tee up several golf balls in a row and tell the watching crowd how important it is to keep your head down when striking a ball. While speaking, he held his head up, looked at the crowd, swung, and hit every ball far and straight down the middle of the fairway. He also placed one ball on top of another, and used a 9-iron to hit the bottom ball down the fairway. Simultaneously, the ball on top flew straight up into the air and fell into Joe's waiting hand. He performed another trick by lining up three balls and hitting them in rapid succession. As he predicted, the first hooked left, the second sliced right, and the third went straight. At one point, he called for a volunteer to lie face up on the ground. Joe stuck a wad of chewing gum atop the volunteer's right shoe, placed a ball on the gum, and drove the ball down the fairway without damaging either the shoe or the volunteer. The show also included Joe's use of a number of funny clubs to execute serious shots.

Fascinated by the performance, I decided to try some of Joe's golf wizardry. I managed to perfect the trick of hitting a bottom ball and catching the top one, but when I tried to hit a ball off a friend's shoe, I failed. I took a divot. Shoe leather flew through the air, and my friend sustained a very sore, swollen big toe. I think Joe should have said, "Do not attempt this shot at home."

Joe was the master of golf trick shots. I was simply a novice.

We Christians can't duplicate everything Jesus, our Master did. We can't walk on water. We can't feed a multitude with only five bread rolls and two small fish. Nor can we raise ourselves from the dead. So what did Paul mean when he wrote in Philippians 4:13, "I can do all things through Christ who strengthens me"? He meant he could handle prosperity and poverty in a manner that honored the Lord by relying on Him.

Prosperity might make a Christian proud and self-confident, whereas poverty might make him bitter and depressed. In life's so-called good times and rough times, we need to maintain faith in the Lord. He will not disappoint us.

6/ Amen Corner

Augusta National, Augusta, Georgia, has hosted the prestigious Master's every year since 1934. The course was founded by Bobby Jones and designed by Alister MacKenzie and opened for play in January 1933. A section of the course, the famous Amen Corner, includes the second shot at the 11th, all of the 12th, and the tee shot at the 13th hole. The nickname appeared first in a 1958 Sports Illustrated article by Herbert Wind. He may have taken the name from a jazz song called "Shoutin' in the Amen Corner" or "Shouting at Amen Corner." Another possibility is he derived the name from a James Baldwin play. Whatever the nickname's original source, it has stuck with Augustus National to the delight of golfers everywhere.

Amen Corner lies at the lowest elevation of Augusta National. Rae's Creek bubbles along behind the 11th green, passes in front of the 12th green and 13th tee box. The Hogan Bridge crosses the creek at the 12th hole, and the Nelson Bridges crosses it at the 13th.

Some church sanctuaries used to include an Amen corner down front and to the side of the platform. Deacons or elders sat in that section and shouted "Amen" often and loudly during the preaching. Their "Amens" encouraged the pastor and informed the congregation that they wholeheartedly agreed with what the preacher was saying.

Amen corners haven't survived in churches nearly as well as Augusta National's Amen Corner, but it is still good to hear an occasional "Amen" during a sermon, especially when it issues from a deacon or elder.

Revelation 5 depicts a scene in Heaven in which four celestial beings and 24 elders worship the Lamb of God. They praise Him for redeeming people from every tribe and nation by His blood (verses 8, 9). Soon thousands upon thousands of angels joined in the worship. They sang praises to the Lamb Who was slain and was worthy of the utmost honor and glory. At the conclusion of the angels' song, the four celestial beings and the 24 elders said "Amen," and then fell down and worshiped the eternal Lord (verses 11–14).

Perhaps we should brush up on our "Amens" now; we are going to shout many of them in Heaven.

7/ The Elusive Hole in One

My son-in-law Brad recently made a hole in one. I'm sure he will remember it for a long, long time.

I have never made a hole in one, but I would like to someday. I scored an eagle on a par 4 once, but the accomplishment pales when compared to a hole in one. If I ace a par-3 hole someday, I hope it occurs when I play well. It would be embarrassing to frame a scorecard showing a hole in one among a string of double bogies.

I may not have a lot of time left to make a hole in one. As I age, the window of opportunity shrinks, but Otto Bucher's story encourages me to keep trying. Playing the 12th hole at La Manga Golf Course in Spain, 99-year-old Otto saw his tee shot find its mark. He aced the hole.

A hole in one may be the accomplishment of a lifetime of golf, but the Christian life brings us opportunities to accomplish many goals far greater than that of making a hole in one. Furthermore, those accomplishments are not restricted to any age bracket. Moses was 80 when he delivered the Ten Commandments to Israel. Caleb was 85 when he routed giants from Mount Hermon. The apostle John was 90+ when he received the Revelation of Jesus Christ. God does not practice age discrimination. No Christian is too young or too old to accomplish great things for God.

Kenneth Wuest, my Greek professor at Moody Bible Institute in the mid-950s, was advancing in age when he translated the Greek New Testament into conversational English. He used to tell his students, "The servant of the Lord is immortal until his life's work is done."

I would love to score a hole in one before I go to Heaven, but I am more desirous of acing the work God has planned for me to do before I depart this life.

8/ Fly Me to the Green!

You stand on an elevated tee box and, and your knees knock as you stare at the green 1,410 feet below. You are standing on a cliff, atop Hanglip Mountain at Legends Golf and Safari Resort in Africa. To reach the green that resembles a map of Africa, your shot must be accurate and your ball must cover a distance of roughly 900 yards—across and down. It will be airborne for about 26 seconds.

Something else you need to know: you will need to board a helicopter to get down to the green. And if you ace the hole, you can collect one million dollars in U.S. money.

This most unusual par-3 hole is actually the 19th hole of Legends Golf and Safari Resort. It is used as a tournament playoff hole or as a once-in-a-lifetime experience for thrill-seeking golfers. In a playoff against Raphael Jacquelin, Padraig Harrington became the only player to make par on this vertigo-defying hole.

The Christian life holds exhilarating experiences when we seem to reach spiritual heights. At those times, we feel much closer to God and the cares of a complex world seem far below us. But we must not become so heavenly minded that we are no longer any earthly good. Jesus took three of His disciples to the top of a high mountain and then transfigured Himself in their sight. The glory of His deity shone from His face and transformed his clothes into dazzling white. Peter wanted to prolong this mountaintop experience, and suggested the group build shelters there. But the experience would be only fleeting; people with desperate needs were waiting for them to come down from the mountain (see Matthew 17:1–15).

Have you noticed that Christians who accomplish great things for God have their hearts and minds focussed on Heaven while their feet are planted firmly on the ground?

9/ How Much Would You Pay for a Golf Ball?

Are you a collector? My collection of logo golf balls, wood-shafted golf clubs, and scorecards isn't huge, but it is big enough to raise the question, "What am I going to do with all this stuff?" The older I get, the more inclined I am to say no to catalogue listings of golf antiques. I do wish, however, I had kept a few Silver King golf balls from the late 1940s.

If you keep your Titleist® for two hundred years, it might be worth hundreds of dollars. I saw an ad for a vintage golf ball priced at $750. It was a gutty ball with patterned composition, and it was in mint condition. The thought of purchasing it failed to enter my mind.

We have all discarded or lost items in the past that would carry a big price tag today. You may be thinking about those old baseball trading cards your mother tossed out when you entered college. As we grow older, we tend to see greater value in what we used to take for granted. We especially attach greater value to significant relationships and memories. We value that old photo of Ben Hogan, but the photo of Mom and Dad is priceless now that they are gone.

As time passes, I find myself attaching greater value to

- Memories of my Scottish parents. They never lost their brogue or their love for my brothers and me.
- My wife of more than 50 years. She has been alongside me in ministry in two countries and five states, and she has never objected to my playing golf.
- Our son, our two daughters, our two sons-in-law, and our granddaughters Jessica and Kayla.

- My salvation. God forgave me and entered my name in the Lamb's book of life January 18, 1952.
- Christian friends, many of whom call me "Pastor."
- Citizenship in a free nation.
- Good neighbors.
- The privilege of serving Christ.
- The prospect of Heaven.

What do you prize most highly? It may be time to take an inventory of your "valuables." Are the price tags accurate? Read Matthew 6:19-21, and see whether you need to switch a few tags.

The Back Nine . . .

10/ Rex and Rudy

When I caddied in the late 1940s and early 1950s at the St. Catharines Golf Course, St. Catharines, Ontario, I most enjoyed caddying for Rex Stimers, who usually played with Rudy Pilous. In those days caddies sat in the caddy shack until the caddy master assigned them randomly to golfers. But a golfer could request a caddie by name, and Rex often requested me in spite of the fact that I was one of the youngest caddies. I was about 13 or 14 when I caddied for Rex most often.

Rex was a popular sports announcer for our city's radio station, CKTB. He was best known for his animated broadcasting of Junior OHL (Ontario Hockey League) games. Our home team was the St. Catharines Teepees. Some of the Teepees advanced to the National Hockey League.

Rudy coached the Teepees, and then became the coach who led the Chicago Blackhawks to the Stanley Cup Championship in 1961. He was inducted into the Hockey Hall of Fame in 1985. A lefty on the golf course, Rudy matched up against Rex quite well, and both had a terrific sense of humor that took the drudgery out of caddying.

Both men treated me well and introduced me to hockey players who joined them on the course. Rex even treated me to rounds of golf at courses near Toronto and Niagara Falls, New York state. It was not unusual to hear him mention my name, Jimmy Dyet, on his nightly sports broadcast.

Both men departed this life a long time ago, but I cherish good memories of them.

Men can have a lasting influence on kids for good or bad. Christian men can choose to mold kids into young men and

women who will impact their culture for God. We don't have to
be preachers to teach the younger generation to do right and to
honor God. We can demonstrate righteousness on the golf
course, on a hockey rink, on a baseball diamond, on a basketball
court, or in a classroom—wherever kids need role models.
Proverbs 22:6 counsels, "Train up a child in the way he should
go, and when he is old he will not depart from it."

11/ The Goofy Ball Ruse

It seems every pro marks his ball on the green. After marking it, he picks it up, turns it the way he wants it, outs it back at the right spot, and putts. I'm sure he doesn't go through this routine because he suspects another player replaced his ball with a goofy ball. A competitor would never stoop to such trickery. But you and I may be subject to the old goofy ball stunt at least once.

A goofy golf ball looks like a regulation ball, but when a player strikes it, it zigzags in a crazy motion and rolls far off line. The stunt is good for laughs, but the unsuspecting player may think he is overdue for an eye exam.

What makes the goofy ball zigzag? I have never cut one open to find out, but I am fairly certain I would find a smaller ball inside the goofy ball.

The Bible presents straight teaching we can believe and follow, but many "goofy" teachings lie at the foundation of false religions. Whoever follows those teachings will zigzag away from the path of truth.

Here are a few false teachings we should never embrace:

- All life is the product of evolution, not creation.
- If God exists, it is impossible to know Him.
- The Bible is simply a religious book written by religious men.
- The Bible is fairly reliable, but it contains numerous errors.
- Jesus was a good man, but He was not God.
- Jesus did not perform real miracles. He was a master illusionist.

- Jesus never intended to die.
- Jesus did not rise bodily from the grave, but his spirit of love lives on.
- Heaven is attainable by human effort.
- Death ends everything.
- Reincarnation awaits all who die.
- A spark of divinity dwells in every human being.

Paul urged young Pastor Timothy to propagate the Truth, and predicted that some undiscerning people would pursue false teachings. He described them as having "itching ears," and said they would "be turned aside to fables" (2 Timothy 4:3, 4).

Let's avoid goofy balls—and goofy religious teachings.

12/ Falling a Wee Bit Short

In 2009, Kenny Perry would have been the oldest player to win the Masters. After 70 holes he held a 2-point lead. He had not had a bogey during the final round, but then his steady play went south. He took a bogey on the 17th hole and another on the 18th. He, Angel Cabrera, and Chad Campbell were tied at 12 under, and moved to the 16th tee in a sudden death playoff. Perry and Cabrera tied the 18th, but Campbell missed a short putt for his par.

And then there were only two. They played the 10th hole. Perry's second shot went left of the green, whereas Cabrera's second shot landed on the green within striking distance. Perry chipped onto the green, but missed a long putt for par, allowing Cabrera an easy two putts for the victory. Steady Kenny had not been steady long enough. The green jacket was awarded to Argentinean Cabrera.

It was a disappointing day for Kenny Perry, his family, and his fans, but he played an amazing 70 holes.

Following Jesus demands steady, consistent obedience. Unless we stay alert to temptation every day and stay focussed on Jesus 365 days a year, we can stray from the goal of completing life's course as victors. Hebrews 12:1 and 2 spur us on to victory. "Therefore we also, since we are surrounded by so great a cloud of witnesses, let us lay aside every weight, and the sin which so easily ensnares us, and let us run with endurance the race that is set before us, looking unto Jesus, the author and finisher of our faith . . . . "

In life, as well as in golf, we cannot quit when we are ahead. We must keep on keeping on.

13/ Presentation of the Colors

Colors appear profusely on golf courses. Players wear an assortment of golf shirts that include green, yellow, blue, red, and splashes of Hawaiian. When rain begins to fall, out pop the umbrellas in dazzling color. And when a ball lands in a pond or sand trap, you may hear colorful language. A few decades ago, golf balls appeared in such colors as orange, pink, lime, and yellow, but not green for obvious reasons.

I suppose a golfer might be considered a purist if he refuses to play anything but a white ball. He might insist white golf balls were good enough for his father and grandfather and, therefore, they are good enough for him. Or he might harp that colored golf balls belong on a miniature golf course and should stay there. Nevertheless, some golfers prefer colored golf balls. They claim they are easier to find when they hit them.

To each his own, but I say there is nothing wrong with adding a little more color to the colorful sport we love.

There is nothing drab about God's way of doing things. He created our planet as a big, blue marble. From outer space it resembles a big, blue golf ball, doesn't it? At creation, God dabbed, swabbed, stroked, and splashed vivid colors everywhere. We see His vibrant artistry in such objects as brightly colored fish, golden sunsets, purple mountains, monarch butterflies, bluebirds and cardinals, decorative parrots, yellow birds, blossoming cacti, rose gardens, pansies, and strutting peacocks, and people too.

Whether our skin is white, red, brown, yellow, or black, we are the products of God's creative genius, and He loves each of supremely. The children's Sunday school chorus says it correctly and simply: "Jesus loves the little children, all the children of the world. Red and yellow, black and white; they are precious in His sight." He loves us all.

John 3:16 reaches out with God's love to all colors, all races, all nations, and people. This verse, often displayed at sporting events, broadcasts the truth that God so loved the world that He gave His Son Jesus as our Savior. Whoever believes on Him has everlasting life.

14/ The Hardest Thing in Golf

Isn't everything in golf hard? Of course the pros make it look easy, but even they choke occasionally or hit an errant shot into the trees or water. The rest of us run into difficulties far more often and freely admit that golf is a tough sport. Here are a few of the challenges I find most difficult: playing a slice around a tree; blasting out of a deep sand trap; hitting a 1-iron (Yes, I have a 1-iron.); putting from five or more yards from off the green; making a two-foot putt; and as a Scotsman, paying the green fees.

Golf pro Ray Floyd identified what he considered "the hardest thing in golf." He commented about it after winning the Senior Tour Championship in Myrtle Beach, South Carolina, in November 1994. During the competition, he had trailed Jim Albus by six strokes at one point, but by the end of the next ten holes he had evened the score. Thirteen holes later, he won the Championship. Ray volunteered: "The hardest thing in golf is playing with a big lead. I know. I've been there. He [Jim Albus] was the only on the golf course with any pressure on him."

If you and I ever think we have a big lead in the Christian life and nothing can defeat us, we are in big trouble. The pressure is on, and it is the hardest time to maintain a victorious faith.

Surely no one would have guessed Elijah would go from hero to zero so soon after defeating the prophets of Baal at Mt. Carmel. His faith dropped from an all-time high to an all-time low when enraged Queen Jezebel put a contract on his life. (See 1 Kings 18 and 19.) He discovered to his dismay that the hardest thing in the life of faith is to hold on to a big lead.

The apostle Paul warned us in 1 Corinthians 10:12 not to feel invincible. He wrote: "Therefore let him who thinks he stands take heed lest he fall."

We need to trust Christ for spiritual victory—today, tomorrow, and every day.

15/ Double the Joy

If you scored a hole in one, your joy must have engulfed the tee box and spread to nearby players. You probably dropped your club, swung a fist high into the air, shouted a mighty YES, received high-fives from your buddies, and performed a spirited victory dance. If you haven't scored a hole in one, I'm sure you will celebrate just as joyfully when you bag your first ace. But what will you do if you score a hole in one on the same hole on two consecutive days? Levitate?

Playing the Regional Foundation Classic at Athens, Georgia, Brendon Todd aced the 147-yard 17th hole on two consecutive days in 2009. By doing so he made nationwide tour history.

The apostle Paul didn't play golf. The game had not been invented yet, but he experienced more joy than a hole in one brings to a golfer. Nothing could rob him of the joy he derived from Jesus Christ. Philippians, a New Testament epistle (letter), has often been called, "the Epistle of Joy," because it frequently uses the words, "joy and "rejoice." If you think Paul wrote Philippians from a luxury penthouse overlooking a sandy Mediterranean beach, think again. He wrote it from a dreary place of confinement in Rome, where he was a prisoner of the Roman Empire. His crime? He had preached the Good News of Jesus.

Shackled, manacled, and guarded by elite Roman soldiers, Paul told the Philippian Christians he was praying for them "with joy" (Philippians 1:4). He rejoiced in Christ Jesus" (3:3) and urged them to do so. As a matter of fact, he repeated this exhortation. "Rejoice in the Lord always," he advised, and then repeated the exhortation: "Again, I will say, rejoice!" (4:4).

Various trials will strike us as we journey through life, but none can steal our joy if we take each step of the journey with Christ. We may never score a hole in one, but we can experience double the joy every day. If that thought makes you feel like performing a victory dance, have at it!

16/ Better Safe Than Sorry

Comedian Bill Murray hit a very bad tee shot during the first round of the Outback Pro-Am in Lutz, Florida. His ball hooked sharply over a street and struck a woman on the head. At the time, she was in her backyard and watching the tournament. She was taken to a local hospital for observation. Bill was so concerned about her he did not finish the round.

The next day, the woman was watching the second round of the tournament when she was nearly struck again—this time by Tampa Bay Buccaneers linebacker Derrick Brooks.

When she saw Bill Murray step up to the tee markers, she took cover inside her screen porch until Bill and his group had teed off. To his credit, Bill went to the woman and asked how she was feeling. She told him she wanted only Bill's autograph on a copy of "Caddyshack."

It had taken only one hit to persuade this female spectator to move to a safe place the next time Bill Murray was about to tee off. Smart woman! Believers can learn from her action. It is better to flee from temptation than to risk being injured by it. Warned by the Lord to flee Sodom, Lot obeyed and escaped the inferno that engulfed the city (Genesis 19:12–24). When Potiphar's wife tempted Joseph, he fled from her presence and avoided a collapse into immorality (39:7–12).

The apostle Paul commanded the Corinthian Christians to "flee sexual immorality" (1 Corinthians 6:18) and also idolatry (10:14). Also, he exhorted Timothy, a young pastor, to flee youthful lusts (2 Timothy 2:22).

School counselors often advise students to just walk away when bullies threaten them, but when temptation threatens us believers, we need to run away. We need to run—flee—to the Lord our Fortress (Psalm 18:2).

17/ Sign on the Dotted Line!

Many sales reps know that treating a prospective client to a round of golf may lead to a signature on the bottom line. Of course, a rep may never get a signature if he posts a lower score than the prospective client. One research study revealed 90 percent of 401 executives claimed that playing golf helps establish closer business relationships. Eighty percent credited golf as a good way to make business contacts.

Jesus often conducted "spiritual business" in the market-places, in fishing villages, in the countryside, and even at tax stations. He certainly did not restrict His contacts to the temple and synagogues. Wherever He went, He used simple words to address profound human needs and to convey significant truths.

Because Jesus met people on their own turf, He was able to gain their attention, arouse their interest in spiritual matters, and answer their most troubling questions. As a result of His availability and concern, He led many people to salvation.

One example: Jesus met a Samaritan woman at a well. The meeting took place outside a village at high noon, when the sun was blazing hot. She was a social outcast, and therefore had come to the well when other women chose to stay indoors. Alone, she would not have to hear their insults and endure their sneers. Although the Jews despised Samaritans (and Jesus was a Jew), Jesus spoke kindly to the woman and requested a drink of water. In the conversation that followed, He offered her living water and revealed Himself as the Messiah (John 4:13–26). She accepted the invitation by believing in Him. Her joy and excitement were so consuming that she left her water pot at the well, rushed back to the village, and invited others to meet Jesus.

Whoever wishes to conduct "spiritual business" with Jesus may do so at any time and anywhere. The transaction does not have to occur in a church building. It can take place even on a golf course. Have you signed on the dotted line yet?

18/ Invitationals

If you Google "Golf Invitationals," you will find almost 1 million sites. Many of those golf invitationals exist to raise money for a worthy cause. With unlimited discretionary funds, you could register and carry your golf clubs from golf course to golf course and tee it up at invitationals from coast to coast. I don't have that kind of money, and I don't suppose you have either. But it's good to know the invitations are out there.

Occasionally I have been invited to participate and speak at a fund-raising golf outing. I have always accepted the invitation eagerly. But almost weekly a friend invites me to play golf locally, and I welcome each of those opportunities too. To repeat a popular statement, "Even a bad day on a golf course is better than a good day at the office."

Now here is a remarkable fact: the Lord has issued an invitation to everyone to receive forgiveness and accept His forever love. It is the best invitation anyone can receive. Jesus invites us to come to Him—believe on Him as Savior—and thereby exchange our sin for His righteousness and our stress and unrest for His peace. One of His invitations is worded this way: "Come to Me, all you who labor and are heavy laden, and I will give you rest. Take my yoke upon you and learn from Me, for I am gentle and lowly in heart, and you will find rest for your souls. For My yoke is easy and My burden is light" (Matthew 11:28–30). In Acts 16, the Paul and Silas extended the following invitation to a distraught warden: "Believe on the Lord Jesus Christ, and you will be saved" (verse 31).

I don't know of any golf invitational that is free, but it doesn't cost even a cent to accept the Lord's invitation to receive forgiveness and everlasting life. If you thirst for these spiritual qualities, heed the final invitation written in the Bible. "Whoever desires, let him take the water of life freely" (Revelation 22:17).

About the Author

Born in the land that gave birth to golf, Jim Dyet became a caddy in St. Catharines, Ontario, when he was just six years old. Although every bag he carried trailed along the ground, Jim's early love for golf quickly reached a high level. Now in his seventies, Jim still loves the grand old game and plays frequently. He has been the featured speaker at a number of golf outings.

He is also the author of 18 books, hundreds of articles, and nearly 50 Bible curriculum courses. His professional career has included extensive editorial and pastoral experience. He graduated from Moody Bible Institute in 1957, Houghton College in 1958, and pursued graduate studies at Indiana State University, The Denver Seminary, and Louisiana Baptist University. He holds a ThD and DLit from Louisiana Baptist University.

Jim and his wife reside in Colorado Springs. They have been married 53 years and have three adult children and two granddaughters.

Circle Books

Circle is a symbol of infinity and unity. It's part of a growing list of imprints, including o-books.net and zero-books.net.

Circle Books aims to publish books in Christian spirituality that are fresh, accessible, and stimulating.

Our books are available in all good English language bookstores worldwide. If you can't find the book on the shelves, then ask your bookstore to order it for you, quoting the ISBN and title. Or, you can order online—all major online retail sites carry our titles.

To see our list of titles, please view www.Circle-Books.com, growing by 80 titles per year.

Authors can learn more about our proposal process by going to our website and clicking on Your Company > Submissions.

We define Christian spirituality as the relationship between the self and its sense of the transcendent or sacred, which issues in literary and artistic expression, community, social activism, and practices. A wide range of disciplines within the field of religious studies can be called upon, including history, narrative studies, philosophy, theology, sociology, and psychology. Interfaith in approach, Circle Books fosters creative dialogue with non-Christian traditions.

And tune into MySpiritRadio.com for our book review radio show, hosted by June-Elleni Laine, where you can listen to authors discussing their books.

MySpiritRadio